D1575192

CONVERSATION STARTERS, EXERCISES, AND SCENARIOS

HOW TO MAKE

SMALL
TALK

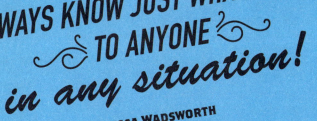

ALWAYS KNOW JUST WHAT TO SAY TO ANYONE

in any situation!

MELISSA WADSWORTH

Adams Media

New York London Toronto Sydney New Delhi

Adams Media
An Imprint of Simon & Schuster, Inc.
57 Littlefield Street
Avon, Massachusetts 02322

First Adams Media hardcover edition OCTOBER 2017

ADAMS MEDIA and colophon are trademarks of Simon and Schuster.

For information about special discounts for bulk purchases, please contact Simon & Schuster Special Sales at 1-866-506-1949 or business@simonandschuster.com.

The Simon & Schuster Speakers Bureau can bring authors to your live event. For more information or to book an event contact the Simon & Schuster Speakers Bureau at 1-866-248-3049 or visit our website at www.simonspeakers.com.

Interior design by Colleen Cunningham

Manufactured in the United States of America

10 9 8 7 6 5 4 3 2 1

Library of Congress Cataloging-in-Publication Data
Wadsworth, Melissa, author.
How to make small talk / Melissa Wadsworth.
Avon, Massachusetts: Adams Media, 2017.
LCCN 2017020013 (print) | LCCN 2017021541 (ebook) | ISBN 9781507204993 (hc) | ISBN 9781507205006 (ebook)
LCSH: Conversation. | BISAC: SELF-HELP / Personal Growth / Success. | SELF-HELP / Personal Growth / General.
LCC BJ2121 (ebook) | LCC BJ2121 .W23 2017 (print) | DDC 177/.2--dc23
LC record available at https://lccn.loc.gov/2017020013

ISBN 978-1-5072-0499-3
ISBN 978-1-5072-0500-6 (ebook)

Contains material adapted from the following title published by Adams Media, an Imprint of Simon & Schuster, Inc.: *The Small Talk Handbook* by Melissa Wadsworth, copyright © 2012, ISBN 978-1-4405-5016-4.

CONTENTS

INTRODUCTION

ASK PEOPLE ABOUT their most embarrassing moment and you're likely to hear stories about how they made fools of themselves in front of people they wanted to impress! Why is that?

The truth is that when cool and sophisticated is the goal, we can often end up being comical and nerdy instead. Part of this is trying too hard and nerves getting the best of us. And being unprepared doesn't help anyone. But the biggest reason we feel so foolish is that we take it all too seriously. There's a tendency to overdramatize the importance of inter-actions in unfamiliar social and business affairs in which we feel we come up short. Mistakes feel *huge*! So huge that you have a hard time forgetting, even years later, that time you referred to the groom by his new wife's ex-boyfriend's name during your congratulatory speech, or the time you asked the adorable guy you had just met what he did for a living and when he said garbage collector you laughed and told him to stop kidding you...when he wasn't.

In the short term, keeping perspective can help manage your frustration level and limit the duration of self-berating. In the long term, having small talk social skills in your repertoire and some mingling mojo at your disposal will give you more communication confidence. It makes all the difference in both the actual handling of any given situation and in the way you feel about yourself.

Everyone longs to be at ease, at their best, in social situations. People naturally want to be viewed as confident and astute in business encounters. Even though some people seem born socially savvy, almost everyone gets nervous from time to time about being in unfamiliar social territory and about making the "right" impression. Preparedness goes a long way to even up the playing field. So does taking the attitude that social and business encounters are opportunities, a game you can have fun with once you know the rules.

In this book we review the basics of being prepared for new encounters whether they are of a romantic, friendship, or work nature. This includes setting the tone with a helpful attitude, being aware of the body language connection, knowing how to naturally engage others with conversational prompts, and being able to politely move the mingling along. *How to Make Small Talk* offers tips for listening, being open and friendly, and knowing when and how much to reveal about yourself. It also explores ideal interaction at work functions and how to get the most out of business relationships.

This book was created to benefit women and men of all ages, who are single or partnered, for use in both work and personal environments. Special care has been given to address issues specific to the following groups or individuals:

- Prospective daters of any age, who are new to, awkward in, or freshly back in the dating scene
- Naturally shy and sensitive people who have trouble feeling at ease or authentic in many social situations
- Social interaction fumblers searching for small talk "dos" and "don'ts" tips
- Career strivers wanting to have greater impact in the business arena
- Tongue-tied romantics who lose their speaking facility in the vicinity of their heart's target
- Lackluster party mixers not getting the results they'd like from their current interactions
- Networking novices wanting to gain tools for successfully obtaining and utilizing business contacts
- Meek minglers ready for a more proactive participation in social encounters in order to gain greater satisfaction from social and business activities
- Business generators honing their communication skills and wanting to expand their opportunities
- Upper-echelon reactors who get nervous around "more important" peers or associates
- Image-enhancement seekers interested in being more intriguing, interesting, and appealing

- Communication enthusiasts always on the lookout for ways to improve and expand their interactions with other people
- New arrivals (to a new town or in a new job) needing tips for creating social connections

How to Make Small Talk is designed as a valuable reference you can use as you perfect your knack for chatting people up and talking about yourself in an appealing fashion. You can master conversational skills that will both put yourself and others at ease and get you taken more seriously. Time to socialize.

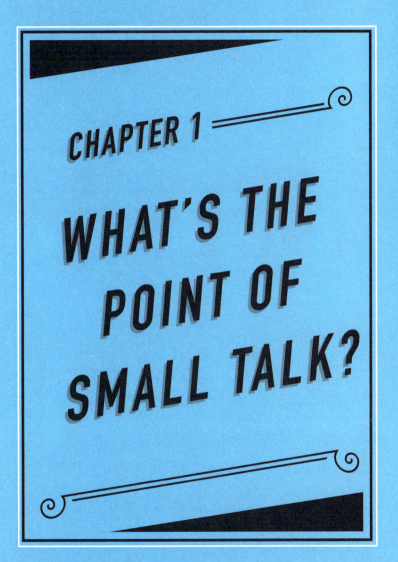

CHAPTER 1

WHAT'S THE POINT OF SMALL TALK?

YOU CAN'T MASTER small talk if you don't put yourself out there. It's necessary to expose yourself to a variety of situations that call upon you to turn strangers into acquaintances, to refresh past acquaintances, and to build upon established relationships. You have to expend the necessary energy to be aware of your surroundings and the people in your personal landscape. Comfortable chitchatting and mingling come with experience and lots of practice. You should find yourself at greater social ease, and enjoying yourself more spontaneously and less self-consciously, as your small talk skills improve and positive experiences accrue.

Successful endeavors are usually the result of a learning process. If you aren't consciously learning, you're probably repeating mistakes. Let's start small.

Small Talk Is Bigger Than You Think

Small talk has often been trivialized and downplayed as surface-speak, a time waster—usually by people who aren't any good at it.

Forget any rocky experiences up until this moment; throw out those bitter labels you've attached to your troubled tongue. Small talk confidence is not as far out of your reach as you might think. You just need to adjust your attitude about how to approach small talk. Small is the operative word here. Little words strung together to open up communication lines between humans. Really, it's no big deal. With a little finesse, small talk can be the tool that expands your circle of friends, increases the satisfaction you feel about your social life, and puts you at ease in various business situations. It can even lead to big deals—such as marriage and new clients.

In our rush from one activity to another, we have only a few minutes to catch up, connect with another person, and relay information.

- *If small talk is done poorly,* we could end up feeling alienated from our peers, friends, neighbors, acquaintances, and coworkers. There's no emotional spark or confidence in the interaction (if done in a real rush, there will be barely a memory of the interaction), and no real meeting of minds.
- *If small talk is done well,* with enthusiasm and true interest, these brief encounters can be the foundation for positive, helpful, and lasting relationships.

Daily modern life does, and can still further, benefit from small talk that creates a helpful network of connections. For instance, we tell friends that we long for a date and they try to set us up on blind dates, drag us off to bars and clubs, or recommend Internet sites for personals and dating. Relay your latest work project topic/crisis and friends or associates listen with interest and provide suggestions that they think may be helpful. They may offer stories about what they've done in similar situations. Or a mother mentions to her child's teacher that her reliable babysitter has moved away and the teacher recommends a neighbor's daughter.

SMALL TALK EXERCISE

DEVELOP YOUR SMALL TALK MUSCLES

The more often you work your small talk muscles, the more responsive they become.

1. Practice on the butcher, the baker, and the candlestick maker. Start by asking advice on their area of expertise. (More about neighborly exchanges in Chapter 5.)

2. Try the topics game. Jot down topics of interest to you and try introducing them into conversation. Start with a "did you know" question or begin by saying "I ran across an article that said… What do you think about that?"

3. Choose a get-to-know target. If you know of someone you find intriguing or that you think would be nice to know better, make an intention to actually do it.

4. Don't hide behind being busy. If you find yourself more connected to electronics than humans, set a monthly goal for social activities.

What do these encounters have in common? The successful ones start with a pleasant "hello" and a smile and very little pressure to perform. Seems simple enough, so why is it that when it matters most, at a swanky party or an important networking event, we clam up or lose our mental capacity for free-flowing thought? *Because in the face of the unfamiliar we become nervous*. This causes self-protective behavior that closes us down rather than opens us up. We silently put up walls that limit our availability, even when we think we want to do just the opposite. Tension is not an energy that's inviting to other people. There are some simple rules for engagement that can be your best friends in any social situation.

We're new in town and we ask a neighbor to recommend a good restaurant, a good dry cleaner, and so on.

Your Small Talk Survival Accessories

First, start by acknowledging that in any interaction there are factors that you cannot control:

- Another person's personality
- What he has on his mind (or hidden agendas)
- His schedule
- The number of people in the room competing for his attention
- The presence of polite and not-so-friendly cliques

There are probably other factors too, but these are some of the most common. The key is to take a few SOS accessories along when you set out to make social and business connections. In this case, SOS stands for:

Self-confidence
Observation prowess
Sense of play

The potential for unplanned consequences is greatly reduced if you know that there is someone caring and loving supporting all your efforts—YOU!

Sense of Self-Confidence

It goes against all our basic instincts to be only minimally prepared when we enter situations in which we don't know the terrain. And yet, it's impossible to avoid being in social and business events in which we don't know many (or any) people and have minimal information about who is hosting the event, how people might know each other, how we might best fit in, etc. The positive way to look at such an unknowable situation is as an adventure. Rather than being intimidated by such circumstances, try seeing the unlimited possibilities in such undefined circumstances.

> **THINK POSITIVE!**
>
> A positive attitude goes a long way. Taking the attitude that each step is helpful, no matter what the individual outcome of any date, party, or work event, should enable you to relax a bit in normally stress-inducing circumstances.

The first rule of self-confidence is to be yourself, your real self. If you don't, it's like arriving only half dressed—frightening indeed. Just as you should pay careful attention to your attire for a date or big social event, you should prep your psyche to match your outfit. Self-confidence is your most effective accessory by far. Yes—interesting jewelry or a great tie may help (more on that later), but it's nothing compared to the aura of a confident or grounded person.

Take stock of your strengths—what you bring to the party, so to speak. People who are unduly uncomfortable in new situations may focus too heavily on their perceived faults. Try this technique: interview yourself first before you get out and have strangers ask you questions. You may want to actually write out your responses to firmly plant in your mind all the things that you have going for you.

1. *What are you good at?* Assess your personality traits, natural talents, and learned skills. This may include particular subjects you've mastered (such as a foreign language), or a personal quality (such as being a good friend), or a talent (such as playing the guitar).

2. *What are you passionate about?* Consider things that you have a current passion for as well as things you'd like to try in the future. Rock climbing or belly dancing, self-improvement or environmental cleanup, Web design or interior design... Take stock and review why they are important to you and what they add to your life.

3. *What are your top two priorities at this moment?* Be honest. This will help you shine in situations that support your priorities. For example, if you answer that building a positive reputation at work is your top priority, then understand that your actions will inevitably support that clear intention. Be confident of this rather than imagining that there are all kinds of pitfalls out there awaiting you.

4. *What do you like to do for fun?* It's a question that will come up, especially in social situations, so know what puts the

joie de vivre in your life. Perhaps you go to car races or like to play tennis. You may go to museums or hunt for collectibles on eBay. Any hobbies? (I know a guy who builds robots, and another who writes and records his own songs.) If you don't have a lot of fun to report, then realize this is an area in your life that needs immediate attention. You could respond: "Going to parties and meeting interesting people" while you work on getting a real, well-rounded life.

5. *What are your favorite things?* Think of categories such as music/musicians, movies/actors, television programs, sports, types of environments (the beach versus the mountains), places to travel, colors, plants/flowers, kinds of foods, architecture styles, to name a few—anything that positively impacts your existence. Just thinking about all the things that you admire and love should put you in a happy frame of mind for a social or business event.

6. *What is the one thing you'd like to change?* This could be a physical aspect such as your height or limberness. You may want to change an exterior feature of your life, such as what you do for a living or where you live. Know what's stopping you from making such a change.

Once you finish your self-review, keep these personal aspects and responses in mind. This exercise should reinforce your confidence level by bringing to light your many positive qualities as well as provide plenty of fascinating fodder for conversation. It may also pinpoint personal areas that you can work on improving for even more self-confidence.

Seeing the Positive in Your Least Favorite Traits

To better accept all your qualities, practice seeing the more positive points of any given quality—which may be valuable assets to skillful interactions. You're more likely to live the beneficial aspects if you make a point of identifying what those are and considering how you might embrace those aspects more fully. Personality traits are not static. You can gently alter how they are expressed. Change is your assurance of this. Here are a few traits that people may feel hold them back socially, and examples of the various potential manifestations of that trait, ranging from negative to positive.

SHYNESS				
NEGATIVE			**POSITIVE**	
Tongue-tied	Blusher	Sensitive	Highly observant	Good listener
APPEARANCE				
NEGATIVE		**POSITIVE**		
Feel invisible	Fidgety	Approachable	Balanced	Control impressions
TRY TOO HARD				
NEGATIVE		**POSITIVE**		
Desperate	Awkward	Opportunity seeker	Enthusiastic	Risk-taker

Observation Prowess

Sometimes we get so self-focused in new situations that we lose our powers of simple observation. That frantic mental checklist is to blame: "How do I look?" "Who do I know?" "Should I get a drink first?" Yet observation is one of your most useful skills at any social or business event. It will work wonders from start to finish. A little initial surveillance enables you to assess the room, to calmly decide on your initial step, and to enter the "action" feeling grounded. During interaction, awareness lets you:

- Assess how you're doing
- Make adjustments
- Try different tactics
- Know when it's a good time to move on as you mingle
- Know when it's time to depart

Taking deep breaths every now and again will keep you calm and give you the two- to three-second lull that you need to assess your interaction. Also, aware-breathing helps you to be present in the moment and more in control of the pace of the interaction. Sometimes we can feel like we have madly dashed through a moment or even through an entire evening—it's that "What just happened?" or "What did I say?" scenario.

A little light surveillance work can also provide you with information for starting conversations:

- "Who's that woman over there in the red dress?"
- "What a great turnout—did you think this party would be so happening?"
- "Great decorations/fun theme. Do you know who is responsible/how they came up with it?"
- "I once went to a party where..."

It's a good idea before going to any event to resolve to keep the observations positive. You never know who's responsible for particular aspects of an event (the food you just criticized might have been catered by the man you're speaking with) or who knows whom. Judgments and putdowns are bad conversation crutches, and not many people are thrilled to engage in negativity for long. You want to generate an upbeat aura, not chalk up bad social karma. And if you meet a person who revels gleefully in seeing how many people she can "cut down to size," she is not someone who will be a positive addition to your circle of acquaintances.

This may go against what you see in sitcoms in which characters throw around witty but slightly or outright cruel remarks and happily dish the dirt. In real life, we don't have scriptwriters directing the action, or laugh tracks, so it's better not to employ negative comments as an entrée to conversation. It doesn't work well at work or play as a long-term strategy, so why get associated with an attitude that has no shelf life?

Sense of Play

For those who get nervous in social situations, being light-hearted can seem like a tough task to pull off. But outlook is everything. Your perception and outlook going into any interaction will greatly determine the outcome. Working it too hard or taking it too seriously can be death to a fluid, fun interchange. Your attitude is transmitted whether you intend it or not. People will subconsciously pick up on it. Trying to be joyful about who you are and where you are, even if you're a bit nervous, helps ensure that you send out good energy.

See where a positive, even downright cheerful, outlook leads. In many ways we are like children each time we learn something new and each time we initiate a new process that is unfamiliar to us from our past experience. The truth is, we don't really know what's going to happen. So, embrace the newness with a child's enthusiasm and curiosity. In social situations, people are generally there to have an enjoyable time, so assume you are part of a happy equation.

Most importantly, manage your expectations ahead of time. Don't go into a small talk situation—a party, a blind date, or a business association luncheon—feeling that if x, y, and z don't happen it was a waste of time. Try considering any outcome as acceptable, and as certainly much better than not having endeavored in the first place.

Small talk confidence is all about baby steps. Take a step, steady yourself, look around, and contemplate the next step. Concentrate on only one step and you have less to fear. Likewise, business networking is about incremental relationship-building phases. It's not realistic to try to build an entire networking structure at a single event.

Begin by being committed to seeing all situations as opportunities:

- For play
- For meeting interesting people
- For expanding your social universe
- For injecting color into your days
- For growing the spectrum of what is possible in your life

The good news is that if you have trouble feeling light and carefree at first, you can fake it until the genuine emotions begin to permeate your performance. This doesn't mean you aren't being yourself; you're merely employing a tactic to curtail those dominating nerves from overpowering all your other great qualities. Think of self-confidence, observation prowess, and a sense of play as personal coaches that help ensure a successful result.

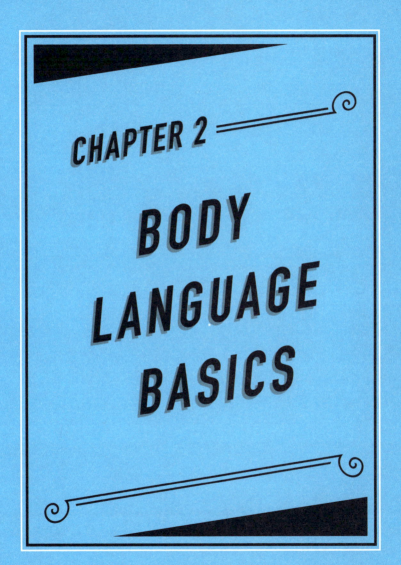

CHAPTER 2

BODY LANGUAGE BASICS

FROM THE MOMENT we lock eyes with someone, or more formally meet them, our body language is sending out messages. Our bodies reinforce and support what we say, communicating even when we're not actually speaking aloud.

Body language can inform us both about the diverse ways we express ourselves and about the commonalities we share in communicating. Temperament shows up in physical signaling.

MEASURING BODY LANGUAGE

One of the reasons that small talk is so effective is that a few words actually go a long way in conversation. How far? Would it surprise you to know that body language and communication experts widely reference a formula (established by UCLA psychology professor Albert Mehrabian in the late 1960s) that states communication is 55 percent body language, 38 percent tone of voice, and only 7 percent actual words? So, actions do indeed speak more loudly than words.

Certain universal body language signals spring out of inborn responsive instincts, according to body language expert Dr. Glenn Livingston, CEO of Psy Tech Inc. and coauthor with Dr. Sharon Livingston of the ebook *How to Use Body Language*. Most people grimace when in pain, smile when happy, and frown in sorrow. Yet many bodily expressions are injected into our repertoire (usually unconsciously by us) via cultural conditioning, individual experience, exposure to other people (especially our families and people of influence), and our distinct personality. Since it has a large learned behavior component, everyone can use body language to purposefully enhance communication effectiveness.

First, become aware of your body language:

- Do you like how you physically move and react in conversation?
- Are you at ease when you enter a room?
- How about when you're interacting with a range of personalities?

If you want to improve upon your unconscious gestures and movements for better communication, start small. Trying too many things at once can look strangely obvious to people who know you, as well as interfere with your ability to listen. It takes practice for the words and conscious body movements to flow together to the point of becoming more organic, composed of both conscious movements and natural reactions. Here are a few basic pointers that any astute conversationalist should be aware of.

From the Neck Up

Begin focusing on body language at face level, where expressions inform. The face is, after all, a highly sensitive barometer that reveals emotions and thoughts in fairly obvious ways. Only someone keen on projecting a poker face will consciously hide intention and emotion (and not be very interesting to interact with unless you're actually playing cards). For the rest of us, the face is full of between-the-lines content, unspoken agendas, immediate responses, and an orchestra of emotions.

Our faces may betray us on those occasions when it's not to our advantage to have our feelings plainly revealed. Hiding distaste or dislike can be a challenge. And yet in the course of human relations it is more often an advantage to have an animated face rather than an inscrutable one—a feat most people can't pull off regardless. Know what to look for and what to express facially as you begin decoding the language of the body and then start practicing incorporating helpful aspects.

See Eye-to-Eye

Eyes are said to be the windows of the soul. At the very least, they can tell you whether someone is speaking from the heart. Also, the eyes are wonderfully expressive indicators of comfort level and degree of interest.

➤ WHAT TO DO

Maintain direct eye contact. This is important in order to establish a connection with someone, to show respect, and to make others feel comfortable. Eye contact indicates that you are interested in another person or what he has to say. Generally, maintain eye contact for about two-thirds of the time you spend in conversation. Less than that and you run the risk of communicating that you are uninterested, uncomfortable, distracted, or even lying. A good listener typically maintains more eye contact than the speaker, and people rarely hold eye contact for longer than two or three seconds before glancing away.

Use your eyes to reinforce the intent behind your words. Eyes are expert conveyers (in concert with brows) of emotions such as concern, gratitude, puzzlement, fear, fascination, questioning, pleading, and joy. Consciously or unconsciously we look to the eyes to ascertain whether what we hear is true. So it's wise to be sure that our own communiqués are reinforced with the eyes.

Let your smile reach your eyes. Laughing eyes and twinkling eyes are highly appealing because they indicate an abundance of happiness or mirth. When people are excited, they widen their eyes and the pupils dilate. Therefore, the eyes can be highly effective for gaining attention for both your verbal and nonverbal messages. The charming flirt knows how to use his or her eyes to advantage.

➤ WHAT NOT TO DO

If you're in conversation, don't scan a crowd or watch people coming in the door over someone's shoulder. A twitching or darting eye may be seen as a lying eye (don't let dry contacts send the wrong message). People blink frequently when they are anxious, scared, bored, or tired, according to the late John Stern, PhD, a pioneer in research on blinking.

Read My Lips

Lips are highly user-friendly for putting others at ease. Sometimes all it takes is a simple smile. And yet it seems that many of us have gotten into the habit of conserving our smiles. We save them for "safe" recipients we're fairly sure will smile back. We save smiles for when we have the time. It may seem silly to those who always have a smile on their face, but some of us need more practice to naturally respond with a smile to a range of situations. Instances in which a smile would be helpful include:

- When you desire to show encouragement
- When you want to be silently supportive
- To reflect obvious gladness to be in someone's company
- To speed along the process of someone warming up to you
- When you'd like to be seen as charming
- To indicate a fun-to-get-to-know nature

➤ WHAT TO DO

Smile at people. It doesn't matter whether you are exchanging words or not. Smile as you pass strangers on the street, smile when you meet with colleagues, smile when you enter a room at a social function. It will become a more integral part of your demeanor. If you do this enough, your smile may even become a key part of how people think of you. A smile automatically communicates interest in other people. In return you're likely to be perceived as approachable, friendly, and confident.

A few essentials about other "lip shtick" you should consider:

- Wet your lips and part them slightly and you're conveying sexual interest. That's strong language so be sure you're using it on the intended person.
- Pursed lips convey disapproval.
- Anger is evident in compressed lips.
- Thoughtful lips twist to one side.
- Biting your lips shows nervousness or anxiety.

➤ WHAT NOT TO DO

Don't avoid smiling or displaying emotion. You'll end up coolly alone or will attract all the wrong types (e.g., people who see disinterest as a challenge or people who can't tell cool from codependent). Miscommunication is the name of that game. Brave showing a bit of your true self; it's your best long-term strategy.

Heads Up

The head and neck combo is very adaptable to nonverbal communication. We nod approval and agreement, and to indicate that we're paying attention. We shake our head "no" to indicate disagreement or disbelief. When we keep a level head we are in control, self-assured, even authoritative. A tilted head is more relaxed and friendly. Head tilts to one side express thoughtful consideration and show active listening. A tilt one way and then another may correlate to asking a question. We tilt our head, bringing our chins down for emphasis, when making statements such as "I just don't get it." We throw our heads back in laughter. And a flip of the head (hair) is a standard flirting motion.

➤ WHAT TO DO

Use nonverbal cues when you're the listener. Leave a favorable impression by receiving the other person's remarks with visible interest. Show that you are in sync with what they are saying. A nod of the head every now and again accomplishes this simply and quite effectively. You can subtly mimic the speaker's head movements—maybe by tilting your head to one side or the other, or raising your chin. This is called mirroring (more on that later) and further reinforces that you are on the same page.

➤ WHAT NOT TO DO

Don't hold yourself stiffly without making head movements; relax your neck and shoulders. When you don't send body language signals for others to receive, consciously or unconsciously, you make them uncomfortable, even nervous. You don't want to come off as zombie-like.

Now Hear This!

Vocal cues have a major role in accurate and compelling communication. All you need to do is watch a child/parent interaction involving discipline and you can pretty plainly see the huge role tone of voice plays in the message that the child receives. Good debaters excel at controlling the tone and tempo of a conversation. Effective communicators pluck from the wonderful range of vocal "keys" at their disposal.

RELAX

Words are only 7 percent of what is conveyed during a conversation; 38 percent is tone and intonation. Relax into letting your voice flex its natural vocal range. This is especially important if you have feelings of not being effectively heard. By being vocally more assertive and using ear-catching intonation, a few words will go a long way.

➤ WHAT TO DO

Practice matching your tone to the intent behind your words. Try reading out loud to hear how you sound to yourself. Experiment with modulating your tone to include high, midrange, and lower intonations. This will help to ensure that you keep listeners engaged and that they "get" the true feelings behind your words.

Use voice tone to accentuate what you say, but without startling the other person. Show excitement if you're making a strong point or relaying a great story/joke:

- "That's hilarious! It reminds me of the time..."
- "I can't believe you said that! I've always thought that too."

Use a lower tone and lean in toward a person to reinforce your interest and enhance the possibility of emotional closeness. Alternately, we inherently want to keep our distance from people we don't like or when we want to clearly communicate a lack of interest or disinclination to share "space" with another.

> **MAKING A POINT**
>
> Expressing yourself with palms facing downward is generally viewed as a more assertive or aggressive movement. Often people will lay their palms flat on a table for emphasis or repeatedly raise a hand up and down to make a strong point. Some people use a chopping motion with their hand to reinforce the idea that "this is the way I believe business works best," or a "this is the way things are" kind of sentiment.

➤ WHAT NOT TO DO

Don't talk too loudly or too close to someone. Nothing is more off-putting than someone you are in close proximity to talking at a high volume. And don't talk too quietly either. People shouldn't have to struggle to hear you.

Hand in Hand

The hands are amazing instruments of communication. You don't have to be a palmist to glimpse people's personalities from the way they use their hands. From the wave of a hand to the handshake, from fidgeting to a light caress, there's clear meaning in those hand gestures. (I'm sure most of you can think of a few not generally displayed in polite company.) Everyday words in the English language point up the positive use of the hands: hands-on, handily, and handy.

POETIC PRAISE FOR BODY LANGUAGE

Throughout the ages, literature and songs have celebrated the power of individual body parts to speak volumes:

> "An eye full of gentle salutations—
> and soft responses..."
> —LAURENCE STERNE

> "Did not the heavenly rhetoric of thine eye,
> 'Gainst whom the world cannot
> hold argument,
> Persuade my heart to this false perjury?"
> —*LOVE'S LABOUR'S LOST*, WILLIAM SHAKESPEARE

> "She is Venus when she smiles;
> But she's Juno when she walks,
> And Minerva when she talks."
> —BEN JONSON

➤ WHAT TO DO

Use a firm grip. This conveys a healthy confidence and sincere pleasure in meeting someone. Be wary of the person who turns your vertically extended hand over flat so that the top of your hand faces the ground and their hand is on top. This person is aggressively declaring: "I'm dominant here; I'm in charge." It's an inauspicious way to begin a conversation or a genuine two-sided relationship. This person is not overly concerned with equality.

To convey openness and friendliness, talk with your palms facing somewhat upward. Some people touch their palms together to emphasize a point. Tossing your palms up may accentuate feelings of humility or uncertainty, such as an "I just don't know" sentiment. A hand or both hands extended toward a listener or listeners can reinforce a call for support.

Be aware of the other person's gestures. This makes it possible for you to show with your own mirroring gestures that you understand their attitude or the corporate climate. For instance, if superiors use their hands as they talk, in all likelihood they will be receptive to you doing the same.

Touch in a nonthreatening way—a light touch of the hand, a brush against an arm—to show romantic interest and encourage a like response. Appropriate context is important for touching. When you initiate physical contact, observe the reaction: surprise, acceptance, reciprocation, or withdrawal. Does the person maintain the distance or move back? Interaction is a two-sided dance. Make sure you're not all about "advancing" your goal rather than engaging in leading and following, acting and responding.

Don't use your hands so much that you distract people from what you're saying. Wringing your hands, clutching your forearms, or obviously not knowing what in the world to do with suddenly awkward appendages called hands will make you look nervous and tense. Some nervous gesturing can be read as lying too.

All Arms and Legs

Arms convey whether you are approachable or off-limits:

- Arms comfortably by your sides or behind your back say that you are inviting connection.
- Arms in a relaxed manner indicate ease with interaction.
- Wide open arms are an invitation to a hug.
- Arms crossed, especially across the chest, communicate a restricted availability.

➤ **WHAT TO DO**

Be aware of your natural conversational style. In conversation outgoing people are more likely to use big gestures, while quieter personality types tend to limit their gestures. Evaluate yourself:

- Are you being too in control or using too little space?
- Could you be a more effective speaker by increasing arm motions to emphasize your enthusiasm, to connect to someone, or to make a point?

- Do you use your arms too much and need to tone it down?
- Have you ever accidentally hit people standing in close proximity?

ARMS AND LEGS ARE FOR FLIRTING

Not only are arms great for hugging, they can be assets in getting a romantic spark going. In flirting, a woman might expose her wrist in the wave of a hand as she speaks or as she holds a drink. This speaks to being open, vulnerable, and available.

Crossing and uncrossing the legs slowly is in almost every flirt's repertoire. Stroke the thighs at the same time and you are inviting touch, and communicating: "Wouldn't you like to touch me like this?" To show interest, face your knees toward the person of attraction.

➤ WHAT NOT TO DO

Don't put your elbows on a tabletop and tap your fingers, fidget, crook your arm to look at your nails, or tightly intertwine fingers. Such movements convey unappealing things like: "I'm impatient," "I'm restless," "I'm bored," or "I'm tense." When you are speaking and you see these physical signals being made by the listener, pause so that she can speak, or ask for her input.

Legs have the square-inch advantage. Because there is generally so much real estate involved, leg positions get noticed, positively and negatively. Who can forget the *Basic Instinct* scene in which Sharon Stone crosses and uncrosses her legs as a power play that ensures all eyes are riveted on her? Alternately, taking up lots of physical space can also be perceived as inconsiderate.

➤ WHAT TO DO

Keep your legs uncrossed. Repeatedly crossing and uncrossing your legs shows impatience or nervousness and can be distracting. Tapping the toes, ditto. In business it's recommended that you keep legs uncrossed or crossed at the ankles for women and lean forward a bit. Only cross your leg with a foot resting on the knee if you're in a casual situation and only if you're male.

➤ WHAT NOT TO DO

Don't stand on one leg—either with the other foot on top of the standing foot or entwined around the standing leg. This displays insecurity and discomfort in standing on one's own two feet. It's difficult to feel grounded in this stance, which puts you at a disadvantage in a social or business situation in which you want to be ready to take action or react to what is happening in a fully present manner.

Avoid rocking or standing in an impatient manner, such as standing with one or both hands on a pushed-out hip, or having one leg placed farther forward with a tapping toe pointing outwards.

Posture and Poses

Standing up straight is immensely important to a positive image. Good posture with shoulders back and head held high presents most everyone in the best light. It is a welcoming stance, and indicates confidence. Someone who stands tall and pushes out his chest is looking to increase his sphere of influence, to literally make a "bigger" impression.

➤ WHAT TO DO

Keep your chin and head up. This helps you stay positive and to be received that way. Looking down, you can get lost in negative thoughts and literally lose visual contact with the other people in a room. At a party or business event, let your walk and your body help you project the attitude that you're an asset to the gathering.

Choose a person to focus on and turn toward him or her. Turning toward someone also puts you in a good position to initiate additional closeness such as leaning in toward him or her, and knee and leg touching if you are sitting or arm touching if you are standing.

➤ WHAT NOT TO DO

Don't slouch. Slouching communicates weakness, lack of stature, and insecurity. Bad postures show a lack of "spine." Leave the hunched shoulders at home. But don't go too far in the other direction, either. A rigid body posture is plainly uninviting as it communicates feelings of inferiority or anxiousness.

Some poses are body language one-liners—nothing subtle going on at all. For instance, hands on the hips and legs firmly planted brags of superconfidence, a take-charge attitude. Crossed arms and a sidelong glance with a raised eyebrow plainly expresses that "I'm not buying this." Men use poses that flex their muscles when they want to show off and clearly indicate sexual attraction, just as a woman may sit or stand in a way that emphasizes what she considers her most appealing body part.

Mirroring or Synchronizing with Others

Mirroring is basically following someone's lead in terms of tone of voice, hand motions, leg or arm positions (crossed or uncrossed), head tilts, and so forth. Used effectively, mirroring is meant to send a message of flattery, a supportive way of showing that you are in sync with another person. In business, mirroring can send a subtle message that you recognize the dynamics of the group. In an interview it may help you be perceived as a good fit for an organization.

Use intentional body language cues in various contexts and see what a difference it makes to the quality of your interactions. Enhanced body language awareness should help to put you at greater ease in social situations, and help you create tighter connections with people. With practice and time, you'll find yourself more persuasive and confident.

What body language won't do is put a good face on a bad attitude. Not many people will be taken in by a big smile if the true feelings behind the smile are negative. If you try to use body language cues to misrepresent your genuine feelings or to stand in for authentic beliefs, you will probably come off as false.

A WORD OF CAUTION

Don't try to mimic every move a person makes. The most important thing to remember about body language is that it must be taken in context. It should be weighed against other factors such as the specific situation, the personality of the person, the actual words, and what your instincts are telling you. These elements should support the body language signals you pick up. Take into consideration your relationship to the person. You may need to consider what other dynamics are going on during the interaction as well as any cultural and gender differences that affect body language perception.

That's the great thing about body language: it can be extremely helpful in communicating true feelings, but it generally doesn't provide a very good false cover for fakers with less than honorable intentions.

CHAPTER 3

SMALL TALK
STYLES

AS CHILDREN, WE learn how to socialize first within the family dynamic and then in our neighborhoods and at school. We try out social skills as part of a group before we advance to one-on-one encounters. Ideally, this progression goes smoothly and helps to instill us with self-confidence and a lively sense of adventure in our social relations.

On the other hand, if your family tended toward dysfunctional interaction or your peers embraced a rebel or outcast identity, you may have a few oh-so-minor lapses in your social education. And, of course, personality plays a significant role in interpersonal communications. But whether you are correcting less than helpful life experiences or looking to improve upon your inborn social nature, awareness and practice are your best allies.

Evaluate Your Social Skills

How do you feel about your social skills? Up to this point we've discussed small talk strategies and body language skills that you can take along with you on social activities. Just like a hostess gift you arrive with, everyone has something valuable to bring to the party in terms of attitude, conversation style, personal revelation, and response to others. It's important to know your strengths and weaknesses in these areas so you can focus on specific ways to refine or glam up your social panache. Keep in mind whether you're bringing a desirable asset to the party or something better left at home.

SMALL TALK EXERCISE

ASK SOME QUESTIONS

Some clarifying questions you should ask yourself include:

Attitude—Do you try to be positive or do you bring whatever you are feeling to the occasion with you? Do you believe in your ability to create social opportunities or do you see interaction as out of your hands or primarily fate driven?

Physical presence—Generally, how do you feel about the way you look? Would an updated hairstyle or wardrobe boost help put you in a better frame of mind for socializing? How do you carry yourself? Are you aware of using your body (walking, gesturing, etc.) to reinforce your presence and messages in a social setting? Do others tell you they value your presence (at work, as a friend, or as a bright light in the world)?

Conversation style—Do you enjoy chatting for hours or prefer more limited talk time? What do you enjoy talking about? Do you keep up to date on current events and news topics? Are you a good listener?

Personal revelation—Are you comfortable talking about yourself? Some people can reveal just about anything about themselves and their families with no apparent self-consciousness. Other people are more apt to put a happy face on all their disclosures. Do you easily talk about your skills or expertise? Are you honest with yourself and others?

Response—How do you respond to others? Do you think that you're perceived as kindhearted, empathetic, supportive, or nonjudgmental? Are you complimentary of others?

Reviewing these essential personality areas can be insightful for you. We can get into a pattern of thinking about ourselves as one "type" of person. Often we too harshly judge our perceived personality type and think of it as unalterable. We're each so fantastically multilayered. To a great extent, we choose which aspects of our total personality we try to bring out or to show at any given time. Examining your traits in a more positive light, you may find that being more of a good listener and less a lead talker can serve you well in your relationships, as long as you don't hide behind the listening role. While our essence doesn't change, life circumstances and experiences do color our personalities for good and bad. Reviewing one's strengths and weaknesses is not for the purpose of self-judgment. It's for clarity, so you can focus on the particular steps that will help garner the results you desire.

Recognizing Your Conversation Style

To help you identify your current conversation style, take this brief, just-for-fun quiz. Don't worry about the results; if you don't like your conversational style, I'll show you how to change it. But for right now, let's just see how you communicate with other folks.

SMALL TALK QUIZ

IDENTIFY YOUR CURRENT
CONVERSATION STYLE

1 What phrase sums up your attitude about social interactions?
   a Life is a stage and I'm the star.
   b What's not to like?
   c I'm all ears.
   d I like to watch.

2 Who are you conversationally?
   a You tend to hold court, leading a conversation and keeping your audience enthralled with your life dramas or uproariously laughing at your wit and humor.
   b You enjoy conversing and can find something to say on most subjects.
   c You are a good listener, interjecting comments judiciously when you think you have something pertinent to add.
   d You're more comfortable letting others do the talking.

3 What do you like to talk about?
  a Yourself and your adventures.
  b Trivia, movies, music, sports, "in the news"
     topics, and people.
  c More meaty topics of discussion such as
     other peoples' personal stories, the role
     humans have in affecting the future of the
     planet, the importance of voting, etc.
  d You're not sure. You usually let other people
     bring up topics.

4 How receptive and responsive are you to other
  speakers?
  a What other speakers?
  b Other peoples' comments keep the conver-
     sation charged and flowing!
  c You naturally make empathetic and support-
     ive comments and responses.
  d You have much you could be saying in
     response to others but few words actually
     come out.

5 What is your conversation goal usually?
  a To be the most amusing and entertaining in
     the room.

b   To help make the conversation lively and interesting.

c   Quality over quantity. Making good connections with a few people.

d   To fit in and not make a fool of myself.

6   How do you feel after most of your interactions?
a   Self-satisfied.
b   Energized and happy.
c   Glad of having met some really interesting people.
d   Regretful that I didn't say more.

Analyzing Your Score: Three or more responses for any one letter (a, b, c, or d) indicates a propensity toward a primary conversational style. You may bounce between a couple of conversational styles depending on your mood and the personalities of the other people you're socializing with (e.g., sometimes you give up the floor when someone else is "on" or to a guest of honor). Keep in mind that just because you currently exhibit one style doesn't mean you can't move toward another modus operandi. To a great extent, everyone has control over the personal qualities he or she projects and how they are perceived.

You don't have to be quiet and meek. You can be quietly friendly. You don't have to be loud and brash; you can be lively and generous. Add up your responses and review these brief definitions of typical conversation styles:

A. The Performer—You seek an audience more than you strive for balanced interaction. You're comfortable in the limelight and can get restless if you're not leading the conversation. Often exceedingly entertaining, you certainly take conversation pressure off the group or your date. Be aware that your social dominance can run the risk of being perceived as narcissistic after a while. People may get bored if they don't feel there's a place for them in the "action." Watch for people's reactions, and practice using your extroverted personality to draw others out and hear what they have to say.

B. Easy Chatterer—You read various publications and are aware of what's happening in the news and with cultural trends, finding it fairly easy to use information in conversation. You come off as friendly and upbeat. Watch interjecting those interesting facts or comments too often or out of context, especially when others have the floor and are trying to take the conversation in a particular direction.

C. Good Listener—While you speak up in conversation, you enjoy really listening to other people, to showing support and letting them know that you are interested. You're seen as empathetic and easy to be around. Sometimes you may be just a bit of a mystery. Appraise whether or not you could be revealing more about yourself, perhaps in order for others to sense a shared connection or outlook, or for others to glimpse a refreshing point of view.

D. Quietly Present—Just because you're not comfortable talking yourself up doesn't mean that you'd rather stay at home. You may try to get out and meet people, but it's just not second nature to you. As hard as it is for you to fathom, people who don't understand your nature may misinterpret your quietness as arrogance or as you being judgmental. This means that you have to work a little harder to enhance your social skills so that you're more vocal. Though you've been quiet in the past, this doesn't mean you can't bring out more of yourself in the future.

While taking a quiz is useful, be sure to use categories like these only as guidelines. Avoid labeling yourself or letting other people label you. No one is all one great personality trait or completely one character flaw. When we stay open to the presence of opportunities (and stop seeing closed doors), we all have the potential to be more fully what we'd like to be.

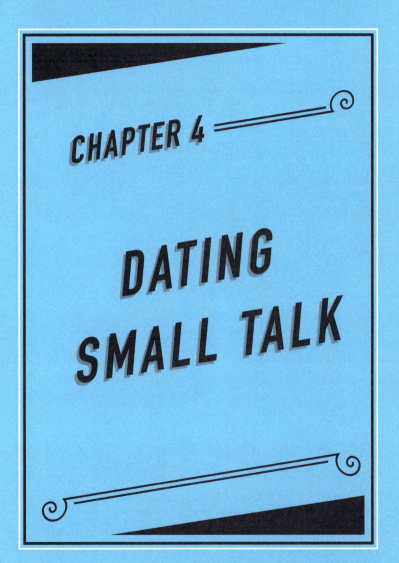

CHAPTER 4

DATING SMALL TALK

DATING CAN MAKE many of us feel at our most vulnerable, so it's easy to get stuck in a pattern of dating behavior that doesn't get great results. In the midst of a date, it can be difficult to turn bad energy around or to strategize about what tactics (short of having a personality transplant) could create a change for the better. Do any of these sentiments sound familiar?

- An alien geek takes over your mind and mouth, forcing you to say all the wrong things.
- Starting a conversation feels about as natural as bathing fully clothed—ill planned and all wet.
- You fervently hope your date has something interesting to say. Why do you always meet people who are as awkward at this as you?
- Being a girly or flirty woman does not come one bit naturally. Does dating have to be this hard?
- You told your date everything about yourself in one night. Then you feel really exposed when he doesn't call back.
- Once a date starts talking about herself, you just let her carry on, without giving much back about yourself.
- You tell your date about your many accomplishments and/or about all the great things you have. But he/she doesn't seem impressed.

The Four Ps of Successful Dating

The good thing about dating is that it plays out in a specific time and place that you have some control over. Whether you have been asked out or did the asking, be sure to supply your input about what activities you prefer and what time of the day you'd like to meet. This helps both parties start off under the best possible circumstances, and neither of you has to end up in an activity that makes you feel foolish. If you're lucky, a date may tap into that mysterious intersection where hopes and desires meet up with fate. So take the time to set the scene.

Plan

Plan an activity that puts you at ease and consider some topics to discuss. A first date between one and two hours is enough time to get to know someone. Being comfortable in your selected situation should help you to be respectful of the other person for the duration—showing interest and being friendly.

Primp

You might want to discuss appropriate clothing if it's not clearly obvious what the dress code will be. Bad breath can be a turnoff even before you get to turn-ons. And too much cologne or perfume reeks of trying too hard and can quite literally make you tough to get close to.

Primping should extend to your living space if you're having your date over to your place.

Project

Project your true personality and interests in a sincere manner, while encouraging the other person to talk about himself by asking open-ended questions. How much is he willing to reveal about what matters to him? Does the answer seem sincere or what he thinks you want to hear? Balance your listening with talking and vice versa.

SHARE TO ADVANCE

Don't squander how much you share about yourself. Letting someone else disclose personal details without sharing your own leaves them feeling a little naked. Some people may be timid and need a little more prodding to open up. But beware of people who get you to talk about yourself without giving away any details about themselves.

Promote

Promote yourself positively. What are your best qualities or talents? How would your best friend describe you? Keep your answers in mind as you interact, so that your nonverbal cues are positive and upbeat. Ask your date a question related to the quality you'd like to share. Then when it's your turn to interject a comment you have the perfect opening.

COMMUNICATION DYNAMICS

Communication dynamics respond well to straight-forward action, but nerves, self-consciousness, and self-criticism often complicate the outcome. The key is to feel increased confidence that you have the tools for feeling in control on the surface. Then, while you may still sense the nerves inside, they won't be running the show.

- Walk tall (no rounded shoulders or downcast eyes) and smile.
- Research shows that women are naturally more physically expressive than guys, gesturing up to twice as often. Understanding this basic gender difference helps ensure more accurate readings of body language cues. The key is context: does it seem general or targeted?
- Once engaged in small talk, maintain appropriate eye contact and face the person you're attracted to.
- Be aware of gestures and postures that give you clues about how you're doing and how your companion is feeling.

The Four Ps provide opportunities for showing how much you give of yourself. While you don't want to overdo it, you do want your date to have an accurate idea about your emotional availability and your ability to give and receive attention and affection.

Action Steps

On a conscious level, communication comprises talking, listening, and responding. Strike a balance between these actions. It may seem unnatural at first, especially if you're used to taking a listening mode.

1. *Ask questions that elicit interesting information.* Yes or no questions create a kind of start-and-stop dynamic. Just as you try to get the small talk going, you ask a question that goes nowhere. Open-ended questions require full answers, at least one sentence long. Smooth conversation flows like a river that progresses around bends, picks up momentum, slows down in places, and passes fascinating scenery. Halting conversation keeps on drying it up.
2. *Listen at least as much as you talk.* Some experts recommend listening twice as much as you talk. Use these as guidelines.
3. *Try to stay flexible to the dynamics of your encounter and respond appropriately to the specifics of your date.* If you're being asked about yourself and you keep cutting your answers short in the name of politeness, you may interrupt the natural flow and exchange of conversation.

Remember, both of you are hoping to hear information that gives real insight into the other person. And eliciting good information naturally provides an opening for you to relate back your own life experiences and interests.

4. *Listen with real interest to what people have to say.* Respond in a way that confirms you are listening. And try to respond to the best individual aspects of a person.

A QUESTION COMPANION

QUESTIONS THAT INVITE ONE-WORD ANSWERS	QUESTIONS THAT INVITE PERSONAL STORIES AND FACTS
"Do you like jazz?"	"What is your favorite type of music/your favorite musician?"
"Is this your first time to this restaurant?"	"I've eaten here before and it's great. What types of food (or cuisine) do you enjoy?"
"Do you enjoy living in New York?"	"What brought you to New York?"
"So you're a chemist. Is that an interesting job?"	"I've never met a chemist before. What attracted you to that type of work (or the industry)?"
"Do you have any hobbies?"	"I've really gotten into wine tasting in the last year. What do you most enjoy doing in your spare time?"
"Does your family live in New York?"	"My family is 2,000 miles away in Florida and I don't get to see them as much as I'd like. Where does your family live?"

Show and Tell and Developing Interest

The weather, the location, the people in the room, and the food you are eating are all safe topics for conversation on a date. Yet beyond the immediate stimuli available to spice up a tête-à-tête there are some additional ways to up your fascinating quotient and to make your date feel likewise engaging. Remember, good energy is contagious and a bad attitude is deadly. If you feel like an interesting human you'll put across a sunnier outlook.

Knowledge is an awfully useful asset on a date. Make an effort to be informed or conversant on a diverse range of topics. This should reduce your own tension in unfamiliar social situations and help you to be perceived as a likable and well-rounded person.

USE THE INTERNET

Having a basic understanding about high-profile persons in a variety of fields refines your conversational finesse. Use the Internet to find out about current social, literary/artistic, political, business, and cultural events that can enable you to reply to a range of questions and to spark conversations. Be careful, though; remember that the Internet contains plenty of misinformation, so do your research thoroughly.

Learn the Basics

If you have a specific "type" of person you'd like to attract or that you have a date with—such as an actor, activist, or athlete—bone up on information about their job or be prepared with questions related to the work.

Take a Class

Night classes and weekend seminars are readily available in most communities. Diverse class topics abound. Not only will you enrich your daily life, you'll be more interesting and have more topics to discuss. You may even find that your new skill will enable you to help someone out with a particular issue or problem they are having in one of these areas. And the classes themselves are great places to meet people who share a common interest with you.

EMULATE GOOD CONVERSATIONALISTS

Go hear interesting speakers. Watch talk show hosts such as Stephen Colbert, Ellen DeGeneres, and Jimmy Fallon. Read interviews that have a question-and-answer format. Interviews clearly show how to take the answer to one question and build on it with your next question. This format also provides examples for following an answer with a comment that reveals something about yourself. Good interviewers provide you with verbal examples of how to validate others and put them at ease.

Dating Dos

The most straightforward goal of a date is to be engaging and likable. The other person wouldn't have agreed to the date if he or she wasn't hoping to have an enjoyable time.

1. *Be joyously confident or nervously confident.* We each have something to offer by way of our company. Know that some of your essence will be glimpsed.
2. *Enjoy the process.* There is nothing to fear because on a date you take one step (an opening question perhaps) and observe what happens, and then you decide on the next step.
3. *Learn from the experience.* As long as you take away something from the date, you're progressing.
4. *Try to reveal a bit of yourself.* A little mystery is good on a date, but you don't want your date struggling to figure you out either.
5. *Take a break when you need to.* This is what bathrooms are for. A few minutes can give you time to ponder your progress or to regroup.
6. *Have positive expectations that a date will go well.* Be open to the fact that a date, and a relationship, can play out in many different ways.
7. *Trust your instincts.* If you feel particularly "right" about someone, go with it. On the other hand, if your instincts are screaming "run!" walk calmly to the nearest exit.

Dating Don'ts

To keep interaction moving along, much like traffic, knowing what not to do can often be as helpful as knowing the right things to do.

1. *Don't always be "on."* To cover nerves, it is sometimes tempting to talk nonstop or to try out all our "best" lines and attention-getting tactics one after the other. After a while it feels awkward to go "natural," and your date may be exhausted trying to intuit your authentic character.

2. *Don't try too hard.* This includes being unnaturally polite, making sure there are absolutely no silences, laughing too often, using profane language, and being too intense or serious. If you find yourself doing these things, take a breath and relax. Think of something you'd really like to know about the person or to comment on an observation you've made during the pause.

3. *Don't lie to impress your date.* You don't want to have to cover your tracks later because you said you had a better job position than you do, more important responsibilities, a higher salary, a famous friend/acquaintance, or the perfect family.

4. *Don't keep your date waiting.* No matter how wonderful you look by taking all that extra time to get ready, it's not polite to keep a date waiting or worrying whether he got the right time or place.

5. *Don't overcompliment.* Everyone enjoys a sincere compliment: "You have a lovely smile," "You have beautiful eyes," "What a great laugh." If your date starts to squirm or looks uneasy, you've gone overboard with the compliments or gotten too personal.

6. *Don't jump to conclusions or make immediate judgments.* A date is a time of exploration. Make sure that you are leaving yourself open to really hearing, and are allowing your date to speak for him- or herself.

7. *Don't forecast failure.* Practice feeling confident—that you have unique insights, information, life experiences, personal qualities, viewpoints, and emotional energy to share.

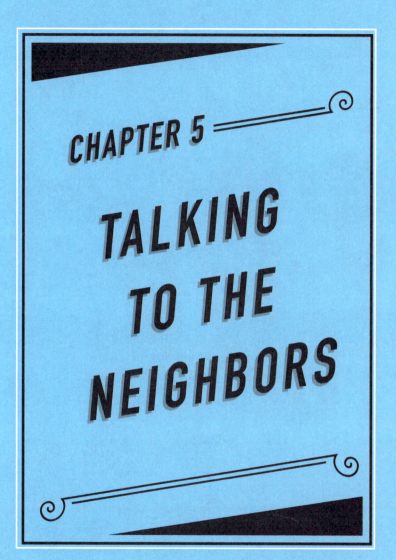

CHAPTER 5

TALKING TO THE NEIGHBORS

YOUR COMMUNITY AND neighbors offer a plethora of opportunities to increase your small talk and social savvy through enjoyable practice, while also making you feel more connected to the people around you. Within blocks of your house, apartment, or condo you'll find a wealth of chances to enlarge your circle of friends and support network, as well as grow your pool of potential romantic partners.

Extending Yourself Around the Neighborhood

Planning, attitude, and attention, as we've said, play major roles in how successfully you interact with others. Small talk smarts become second nature only after positive intentions are enacted repeatedly. Yet modern life offers up many distractions to our best social intentions—both of our own making and stemming from collective community mindsets. Keep aware of potential communication roadblocks in order to limit their effect on your social success. Common hindrances to improved face-to-face communication, to name a few, include:

- Being an electronics junkie—how long can you go without using your cell phone?
- Work overload and life overscheduling—you know who you are.
- A standoffish community personality—pervasive communal attitudes can affect ease of interaction.

- Independent-minded living—modern life often supports the notion of the rugged individualist: each man or woman as a soloist in day-to-day living.
- Assumptions about commonalities and differences—coming to conclusions based on what we see rather than what we know about a given individual.

BEING MORE OPEN

You can't change other people, but you can be more open yourself. Even subtle changes in your approach to people—exhibiting your belief in the pleasure of a friendly "hello" and in the value of getting to know people—can go far in creating positive results.

Recognize that there is a richness of human connection waiting to be tapped. Treat everyone as if no one's really a stranger. Don't throw up nerve-induced roadblocks that are within your control to get past or eliminate.

Potential Roadblock One: Being an Electronics Junkie

So, how socially connected are you? You may have a computer and access to the Internet, a cell phone, and an instant messaging device and may still not be optimally connecting with the people around you. While electronics have made daily life convenient in many ways, these gadgets haven't exactly made us more apt to notice our fellow humans. There's a social downside to communicating in speed dial mode all the time. We can get out of practice with (or never become familiar with) engaging in focused and meaningful interactions up close and personal. For many of us there are fewer quiet spaces ("Can you hear me?") throughout the day for being in touch with what's going on around us.

The following exercises are designed to help you recognize the opportunities for more neighborly connections, as well as help set the stage for the subsequent small talk opportunities that can arise from simple states of awareness and friendliness.

➤ MODERN COMMUNICATIONS—A TRUE-OR-FALSE QUIZ

1. A busy life equals a life of substance.
   ❏ **True**   ❏ **False**
2. Constant cell phone use or instant messaging confers an air of importance or popularity upon the user.
   ❏ **True**   ❏ **False**
3. Electronics keep people well connected.
   ❏ **True**   ❏ **False**
4. If I'm not available 24/7, I'll miss an opportunity.
   ❏ **True**   ❏ **False**

➤ ANSWERS

1. *False.* Busy can have "meat" to it or not. Some busyness is disorganized tail chasing; some is the result of needlessly overextending ourselves; some of us create an inordinate amount of activity to cover for a less than thrilling, fulfilling, or balanced existence (workaholics use this one).

2. *False.* True, electronics give you quick access to others, but since nearly everyone has a cell phone or other communication device these days, the cachet it once had is a thing of the past. Beware of cell phone abuse—talking on the phone anywhere without discrimination or consideration of others. It is not only impolite, it can be perceived as you not being comfortable in your own company.

3. *It depends.* Electronics keep you connected. Whether or not you are well connected is up to you. Well connected is using electronics to stay in touch more often with people you wouldn't otherwise (because you just weren't a letter writer, etc.), or to be more considerate to others (you can call if you'll be late or to inform about your whereabouts). Well connected is employing electronics to reach a greater number of potential business contacts. On the other hand, you are probably not well connected if you use communication devices as a personal shield or distancing device.

4. *In most cases, False.* Hardly anyone is so important that a message won't suffice. Over-reliance on always being "available" may be giving you a false sense of importance. Others could see this as you using your communication devices as a personality or confidence prop. If you can't leave the house or the office without your cell phone ever, reconsider being such a satellite slave.

SMALL TALK EXERCISE

ROADBLOCK ONE OPPORTUNITY: SWITCHING TO AN OBSERVATION MODE

1. The next time you run errands turn off your cell phone.
2. Make a point of watching how other people are interacting with one another. Is there more politeness or curtness? Are people engaged in more than one activity at a time? Who seems to be having the most positive interactions?
3. Did you see anyone with whom you would have liked to have a chat?

SMALL TALK EXERCISE

ROADBLOCK ONE OPPORTUNITY: FACING THE WORLD WITH A SMILE

1. Smile and make eye contact with people you pass on the sidewalk, smile at the person in the car next to you when you are stopped at a light, smile at other shoppers in the grocery aisle or at the mall.

2. Note the reactions of other people. Were they pleasantly surprised? Did they warmly return the smile or say "hello"? Who was afraid to meet your glance or outright ignored you?

3. Notice how an abundance of smiling makes you feel.

Potential Roadblock Two: Work Overload and Life Overscheduling

With all the layoffs and downsizing that have taken place in the last decade it's not uncommon for an employee to be doing the job of two people. We're busy and pressed for time, which can mean less relating to people in a warm, interested, and caring way that is mutually supportive of meaningful interaction.

In addition, some people have gotten onto the "I'm just so busy" treadmill. No matter when you call or talk with them they are running off to do something "really" important or they have another fire to put out. There is a difference between hectic and satisfying. Don't fall into the trap of creating noise in your life that doesn't feed your basic need for real connections. In even the busiest schedule, room can be made for a few minutes of friendly chitchat. A little small talk can really brighten your outlook on an otherwise hectic day.

ROADBLOCK TWO OPPORTUNITY: STEPPING OUT

1. Be aware of who interests you in your building, on your street, or in your town.
2. Make an intention to introduce yourself and find out a bit about them.
3. Follow through. For instance, want to know if that rather attractive someone down the hall is attached? Plan to ask him how he likes living in the building the next time you run into him taking out the trash, working out in the building gym, or going to his car. Want to take it a step beyond? Mention how you're so busy that you haven't had a chance to meet many people, but that you were thinking of having a cocktail party soon to remedy that situation.

SMALL TALK EXERCISE

ROADBLOCK TWO OPPORTUNITY: GIFTING OTHERS WITH GOOD PRESENCE

1. Commit to giving your attention to those you interact with, even if it's only for two minutes. Create the intention to be friendly and polite to people you normally engage rather mindlessly.
2. Ask how their day is going or comment on their job or service.
3. This exercise is intended to provide practice for being fully present and sincere, which is a great way to begin any interaction.

Potential Roadblock Three: A Standoffish Community Personality

Each community, town, and city has its own general personality that may make connecting and interacting with others a challenge:

- Some gated communities don't seem particularly conducive to intermingling.
- Commuting suburbs often present the problem of people going to and from their respective homes right into their various modes of transportation with absolutely no interaction with neighbors.
- People living in cities can become so self-sufficient that asking a neighbor for the proverbial cup of sugar would be unthinkable.

> **MEET PEOPLE IN THE MOST MUNDANE PLACES**
>
> Everyday haunts—parks, grocery stores, laundromats, and so on—make good places to meet people because you're likely to see the same people time after time if you're paying attention. Playfully investigate and be willing to initiate conversation.

SMALL TALK EXERCISE

ROADBLOCK THREE OPPORTUNITY: SPARKING QUICK CONNECTIONS

1. Practice noticing and finding connections around you.
2. If you're a commuter, talk with your co-commuters. Comment on their reading materials or ask for assistance on a crossword puzzle word.
3. If you use a taxi, drivers are nearly always from somewhere else, so ask where they hail from.
4. Take advantage of community events and scheduled get-togethers such as condominium pool parties or neighborhood farmers' markets and art walks. People who live near you frequent such events and are there for a common purpose.

ROADBLOCK THREE OPPORTUNITY: CONNECTING WITH PERSONAL STYLE

1. Make it a point to regularly explore your neighborhood.
2. On your walks, smile, and make it a point to talk to people.
3. Go into some shops you've never frequented and talk to the owners or staff. Ask them about the business.

Potential Roadblock Four: Independent-Minded Living

Sometimes it seems that past generations connected more often with their neighbors, coworkers, and community members. Generations past joined the local country club and fraternal organizations such as the Elks Club. They played bridge and pinochle, and invited neighbors to join them for barbecues and cocktails on the patio.

Today, in general, we're a much more independent lot and much busier to boot. When was the last time you asked your neighbor for assistance with something or spontaneously invited her to spend time with you? These days if a neighbor does something extraordinarily kind it's apt to make the local news. And there are fewer rules about traditional roles and the timing of our life endeavors, so we're not always in sync with our neighbors in our career and relationship phases.

Establishing connections that enrich your life may take a bit more concerted effort. You could:

- Join a book club
- Join an alumni group
- Volunteer for an adult softball or soccer league
- Spend a weekend running
- Join a bike club
- Help out at a local charity
- Enlist in an environmental cause
- Find a single parents group

Perhaps you and a friend could turn a fledging interest into a group dynamic—work together to establish a regular dining club (eating out or taking turns making themed dinners in) or a wine-tasting group. This creates a regular basis for getting together, and for meeting new people as new members join. The great thing about joining a specific group is that you immediately have something in common to small talk about.

SMALL TALK EXERCISE

ROADBLOCK FOUR OPPORTUNITY: INVITING INTERACTION

1. Create an interactive event. This may be a garage sale, housewarming, themed holiday party, or casual cocktail soiree—anything that brings people from your community to your door. You might make a great lifelong friend or you may meet someone who provides another kind of valuable life connection—such as a great masseuse or an investment advisor.

2. Throw a holiday party for the neighbors on your block.

3. Follow up with your new connections to determine who is open to continuing a relationship.

4. Ask people to join you for coffee, to walk dogs together, or to exercise (jog, walk, play tennis, or take an exercise class), if you know they engage in such activities.

ROADBLOCK FOUR OPPORTUNITY: STIMULATING DÉJÀ VU ASSOCIATIONS

1. Join a repeat event such as the annual garden tour, a benefit golf tournament, a run/walk for cancer research, or an annual arts- or music-related event. This provides a structure for building a history with a particular group of people.

2. Work to extend the relationships you create beyond the event. For instance, you could suggest to people who volunteer and work hard for a charity event that they reward themselves afterward by visiting a local spa together.

Potential Roadblock Five: Assumptions about Commonalities and Differences

Sometimes our assumptions about what we have in common with certain people restrict our openness to new encounters. Our assumptions may be based on age, culture, appearance, or lifestyle. Stay open-minded with an open heart. Small encounters like these marvelously layer and "fill in the gaps" of our existence. They can create a cumulative sense of fullness. Be receptive to overtures by others and initiate your own.

ROADBLOCK FIVE OPPORTUNITY: COMPLIMENTARY CONNECTIONS

1. Make a point of speaking with people of all ages, from the kids fidgeting in line at the post office to the older folks in the grocery store.
2. Ask for others' opinions (on clothes, food, gifts, etc.).
3. Offer assistance where it's needed or be complimentary.

SMALL TALK EXERCISE

ROADBLOCK FIVE OPPORTUNITY:
OPEN YOUR ARMS

1. When new neighbors move in, stop by to introduce yourself and to welcome them to the apartment building/condo complex/neighborhood.
2. Take them a thoughtful or helpful gift to help them settle into their new home.
3. Give them a list of neighbors' names with addresses and phone numbers.
4. Provide a list of your favorite restaurants and reliable tradespersons such as electrician, handyman, and plumber.

Your social universe expands proportionately to the energy that you expend. Don't overthink social encounters; rather strive to be the friendly person who walks into a store, and the smiling face that says "hello" on the street. Make time to chat with neighbors. Get comfortable in not knowing or having expectations about where a conversation will lead. By putting yourself out there, by being the "approachable" person in a crowd, your satisfying people connections are bound to grow.

Advancing Your Love of Conversation

Often we get into a rut about with whom, when, and where we communicate. Try stretching beyond habit and comfort zone. Make little small talk strides that enliven your days and enlarge your social world. So often people just need someone else to brave the first word, to make the first move. Be that someone and see what a difference it makes in how you perceive your communication abilities:

- *At the grocery store.* Why waste a good wait in line with silence? Survey what the person in front or back of you has in their cart or up on the counter. Try a friendly "Looks like you're having pasta for dinner," "You look like you're having a party," or "I'm impressed you eat so healthy."
- *In the elevator.* Ah elevators, the land of the blank stare and uneasy space shifting. Yet there is small talk lurking there.

Getting on the elevator, you might comment, "Thanks for holding the elevator, it took me so long to get here this morning, what terrible traffic." Since everyone is in such close quarters it usually takes just one person to make a first move that relaxes the entire group.

- *Around the home and garden.* Bridge that lawn gap by proactively commenting on your neighbor's new plants, obvious green thumb, or golf-course-perfect lawn when you're outdoors at the same time. If they have a little remodeling work going on, ask how it's proceeding.

- *At the gym.* Health clubs can be favorable places to meet people, but use common sense about initiating exchanges. Rather than talking to the treadmill runner, head to the stationary bikes for conversation. People tend to be less out of breath and even read while riding.

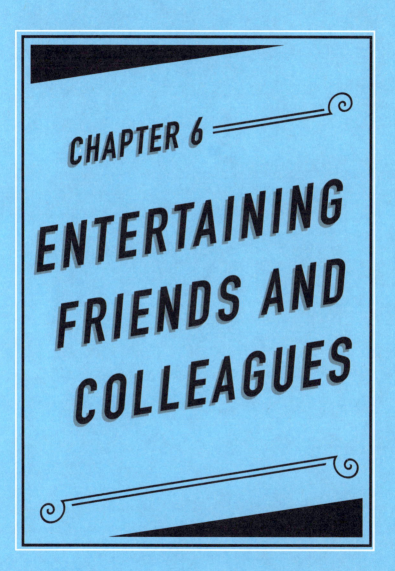

CHAPTER 6

ENTERTAINING
FRIENDS AND
COLLEAGUES

THERE IS NO better way to get to know a few people than over a meal. Dinner parties and luncheons create an immediately intimate environment conducive to forming affable bonds with others. And in many cases these meals present the chance to meet people you might not otherwise know were it not for a host creating a stage: a specific setting, time, and place for the introduction.

Organizing a Dinner Party

Don't shy away from a potentially jovial way to socialize that gives you a great deal of control. As a host you control factors such as the guest list, the menu, the tone (dressed up or casual), and the entertainment. Done well, inviting people to your table is the perfect way to share a satisfying good time.

The Invite

There are three kinds of invitations these days: verbal, written, and electronic.

1. For dinner parties of twelve or fewer, a verbal invite is generally fine. This keeps things casual and is less work for you.
2. If it's a special occasion such as a birthday or some type of congratulations celebration, consider a written invitation that clearly states the reason for the gathering. And, of course, written invitations, with RSVP information, help you to organize larger gatherings. You can include

information about whether the guests will be requested to participate in any activity other than dining (for example, a murder mystery party).

3. Mailed invitations are more personal (and less likely to get deleted or sent to the junk mail folder), but electronic invites are increasingly being used and considered acceptable. Use common sense and the format that you know works best for contacting your particular invitees.

The Arrival and Introductions

As a host, once someone is at your home, making the person feel welcomed is key to his or her comfort level.

● Show her around your home or apartment. This tells her that you have opened your doors to her company.
● Introduce her to other guests to help minimize initial mingling awkwardness.
● Introduce guests by stating their names and one or two interesting things about them: "This is Sally Jones, a good friend from high school and an amazing interior designer." Or: "This is my neighbor John Smith. He just started his doctorate in Civil War history."

As a guest, you can launch small talk by saying something appropriately complimentary to your host, such as: "Lovely food" or "It smells good in here." If the home has been specially decorated for the dinner, comment on it: "Beautiful Christmas tree!" Bringing something more imaginative than flowers or a bottle of wine as a host/hostess gift can make you memorable, and give you something to talk about right away.

If you know that you'll be attending a luncheon or dinner in which you won't know the other guests, you can plan (or volunteer) to be one of the first to arrive so that you can offer the hostess assistance.

Ask guests how they know the hostess or other guests. Observe the interactions as you listen to get a sense of people's commonalities and how they are connected. Do a number of people belong to the same club or go to the same gym? There almost always will be someone in the group who will be warm and welcoming to a guest outside the regular group.

➤ BUSINESS GATHERINGS

Business gatherings of either all coworkers or people from a mix of companies and businesses offer built-in small talk opportunities. Topics you can discuss to create a comfortable atmosphere include:

- Architecture (if you or the other guests are from out of town, local landmarks make a good topic)
- Food and wine
- Traffic/weather
- Travel experiences
- City/country of origin
- Current events/info in the news (so long as you don't stir up controversy)
- How long someone has been with a company

- What they think of the current industry direction or competitive companies
- Who really impresses them at their company or who they think is a businessperson of note
- How they got into the industry
- An important pending company or industry event (such as a company going public or an industry conference)

TAKE NOTES

If you have trouble remembering information you hear, try taking notes after a dinner or lunch. When you get back to your desk or arrive home, make notations about the particular interests of certain people, current life happenings, the names of family members, anniversary dates, and so on. You can use the information later to refresh your acquaintance by asking questions related to the information, such as: "Didn't you close on your new home last week?" "How did your son's hockey game go?" or "Have you been able to get out and enjoy your new boat?" Again, use small talk as a valuable relationship tool that strengthens initial connections.

The Energy/Entertainment

It greases the wheels of small talk to have the "energy" of the event emanate from a focused source initially. Such sources might include:

- The hostess, who makes the introductions and who sets the tone for interaction.
- A guest of honor, whom everyone wants to say "hello" to.
- An event theme, which enhances energy, injecting an aura of celebration or extending an invitation to step outside normal day-to-day behavior.
- A hired entertainer, who creates energy that gets everyone talking.
- Games and other outdoor activities, which go well with backyard meals.

➤ BUSINESS-WISE

At a business meal, the social energy may be generated by the most important person at the event, such as the company president or CEO, who establishes the tone and topics for interaction. In many cases head honchos are looking for a moment to relax and may prefer that everyone carry their own social weight, so to speak. Being aware of the dynamic that exists can be crucial to interaction ease. If you want to single out someone (who is not at your table) for contact, do it between courses or following the meal. Make it brief. For instance, thank the company president for putting on a great event. At a Christmas dinner you might find an opportunity to say something like "Thank you for the wonderful evening. I'm excited about business for the coming year."

At a business event with the purpose of conveying information—whether it's a press conference or a business-specific presentation—that action takes center stage (usually at the beginning of the event) and becomes the source for initial conversation once food is served. If a restaurant meal is really a working session rather than a cordial sharing of food and thoughts, then that is the focus throughout the gathering. Everything else, including the food, is secondary. Make a menu selection quickly and get on with business.

PARTY ICEBREAKERS

Party icebreakers enliven parties and provide an excuse for anyone and everyone to intermingle. Try this idea: Master the Prop—The host/hostess provides various props to guests as they arrive: monocles, fake cigar/cigarette, feather boa, cane, fake mustache, funky hat, belt (Western or sumo), etc. This gives people a reason to speak to anyone; they have a license to get engaged lightheartedly with one another.

As is true for any social affair, business gatherings bring together a variety of personality types. It usually takes some effort on each participant's part to contribute to the flow of conversation. Plan to be proactive about your participation. Business can be pleasure with an upbeat attitude, good manners, and the skills to ignite a little conversational spark.

The Meal

There is a degree of truth that who you sit next to determines your enjoyment of a meal. But remember that everyone is thinking just that, so strive to be the interesting conversationalist and good listener who is a pleasure to be seated next to.

DON'TS

Eating too quickly, overconsuming alcohol, splaying your elbows on the table, and using a boardinghouse reach are common faux pas. If you're not sure about proper etiquette or table manners in a range of situations, consider doing the following:

- Take a class to refresh yourself.
- Purchase a book and practice being genteel with friends.
- Review the basics online before your next business trip.

Manners are part of the script for putting yourself at ease in social situations and for showing respect to your host.

At dinners the host usually determines who sits next to whom. If she or he (or you) does a good job at seating placements, you should have someone interesting—either with a similar background or perhaps an entirely different life experience—to speak with and get to know. You have people on either side of you, so strive to balance your communications with both sides. Perhaps speak with one person early in the meal and turn your attention to the second person during dessert and coffee. Sometimes the flow of conversations from one side to the next flows naturally. At times a topic will engage the entire table. Some hostesses like to have diners switch seats with each course to enable people to mingle even as they dine. The only time you may want to sit quietly is when you are listening for a natural place to enter a new conversation. Otherwise use your small talk skills to draw others out and to reveal aspects of yourself.

➤ BUSINESS MEALS

For a large percentage of sit-down dinners and luncheons either you'll select from the menu or someone else has made the choice for you. On occasion you may have the job of selecting the restaurant. Steakhouses are a perennial favorite with the traditional business crowd, but try to know the tastes of the most senior person at a dinner. They may be a more adventurous diner or happy to break from the routine. If you know you'll be out of town, do research on the Internet to find out about reputable restaurants or hot new dining finds. Then you'll be able to make good recommendations while everyone else is mumbling about not knowing what's around. When you take people out for a meal, you are essentially the host or hostess, so be conscientious about that role. If the meal is definitely all business, be sure your guests are satisfied with their menu options but don't be too distracted by the food yourself. This type of meal is more about creating a forum for discussing some specific business issue.

In the business world, differentiation is good. This concept can extend through every aspect of business including the meal. Context is important in all effective communication, so consider these factors:

- What do you know about who will be in attendance?
- How important is food to the success of the event?

Many event organizers play it "safe" with dull menu choices. In both pleasure and business it is impossible to please everyone, especially when it comes to food—thanks to diets from hell and food sensitivities. You can't know all the food peculiarities of your guests, so aim to create a memorable dinner or luncheon in which the food is a key ingredient that whets the appetite for insightful and fascinating conversation. A good meal nourishes social intercourse.

Following Up and Reinforcing Connections

Always send a simple thank-you note to your host or hostess.

- Mention the aspects of the meal or gathering that stood out to you: the food, the atmosphere, the entertainment, the conversation.
- Thank the host for introducing you to a particular person whose company you especially enjoyed.
- If a colleague arranged an event, send a brief email expressing appreciation.

- Send thank-you notes to potential business partners or clients following an initial meeting.

> **THE POWER OF EMPATHY**
>
> Empathy and compassion go far in social and business situations. If you feel like you need rescuing, rescue someone else instead. Who do you see alone that would appreciate you coming to his aid? Approach him with a smile and say, "Hi, I'm... I don't know anyone and am feeling a little awkward. What is your name?" Engage children if they are present—probably no one feels weirder than them. Embrace your own kind presence as an asset and people will discern an attractive nature.

Relationships die when they aren't attended to. So be creative with how you want to keep a connection alive. It's a nice personal touch to follow up a particularly good interaction with a link to an article or news clipping that relates to a subject of interest that was discussed or touched upon. It shows that you were truly interested and that you would like to grow the connection. Be a standout socializer from beginning to end.

Personal Assets That Rule

In all these social situations the right attitude goes far. Have a sense of humor. It's a social event, not a job review.

Make levity your life preserver. Humorous self-deprecating comments and disarming remarks usually merit a positive response.

Whether it's a strictly social affair or a business-oriented coming together, people respond positively to the same basic cues: a genuine smile, a connected gaze, and a warm handshake. Want to be seen as really amiable and attractive? Fully participate and be upbeat. Make others feel comfortable interacting with you and the reflected glow will put you in a good light.

> "Life is a banquet, and most poor suckers are
> starving to death!"
> —ROSALIND RUSSELL AS MAME IN *AUNTIE MAME*

Talking to Your Boss

Remember that communication is the exchange of information, and bosses love to be kept informed of what's happening, both good and bad. This provides employees with an ideal reason to instigate communication with a superior (following the appropriate channels for communication, of course). Timing plays a role in the positive exchange of work updates, especially if something has changed. Be proactive and responsible. For instance, you might initiate a conversation with:

- "Do you have a minute? I just wanted to give you an update on the Best Life project."

SMALL TALK EXERCISE

USE SMALL TALK AT WORK

We already touched on small talk in situations where entertaining is connected to business. But what about talking to your colleagues in the workplace itself? Good news! All the small talk skills that you acquire in your social interactions easily translate to successful work interactions, with a few modifications. Implement your small talk skills by:

1. Using your observation skills to get to know workplace dynamics.
2. Being yourself. You don't have to be a different person to succeed. Know how to use attitude, play to your strengths, and build up desirable traits.
3. Reducing fears or uncertainties with positive action. Engage in actions that fulfill work responsibilities (helping you to be perceived as reliable), or that contribute to the team effort.
4. Engaging in professional interactions that are genuinely friendly, respectful, and fruitful.
5. Emulating success (another form of mirroring).

● "Everything is going great with the Best Life project. I met with the client today and they expressed how happy they are with the hard work they're seeing on the ad campaign."

Constructive communication includes making sure that your boss doesn't get surprised by a work development. Use a calm manner or tone and be organized with your thoughts when addressing work challenges. Be positive in your communications. Rather than telling a boss why you can't do something, let her know how you can.

Tips for Successful Interaction with Upper Management

Context and personality determine appropriate interactions with superiors and bosses, so always be attuned to such factors. And keep these general guidelines in mind.

1. *Don't always talk about business.* This may seem counterintuitive but upper management talks business all day long. More business talk just becomes part of the blur. So when you run into them in the hall, at lunch, or at a business dinner, approach small talk on a personal level.
2. *Follow upper management's lead.* If business is what they are obviously most comfortable talking about (to the exclusion of everything else), engage in business talk. Perhaps shift the conversation to business on a more general level. Show awareness about how a world event or emerging market may impact your business.

3. *Be upbeat.* Bosses want to hear that you're onboard and they like brevity. After a meeting you might interject comments such as, "I'm optimistic about the new focus for the company" or "Great meeting. I think that the new sales strategies will net good results in my region."

4. *Be in the moment.* Every contact is a chance to make a good impression. Use your attention and body language to convey warmth and respect, and to show you're fully present during quick or prolonged exchanges.

5. *Be authentic.* Comments along the lines of: "I've enjoyed my first few months with the company," or "I always wanted to play this golf course, thanks for making that possible," are acceptable to a boss. Just don't fawn.

6. *Don't fake knowledge or feign interests you don't have.* This can backfire. Why chance looking stupid? If you don't know the answer to a question, say you're not sure but will get back to them with an answer.

7. *Don't interrupt.* Resist the temptation to jump in with a comment when other people are talking, especially with a superior who is used to having the floor. A well-considered thought at an opportune moment is a better strategy.

Coworker Fellowship

Get to know your coworkers just as you would with a neighbor. Be curious and interested. Here you have the added benefit of seeing them nearly every day so there are opportunities galore for interaction and learning about each other. People get familiar with each other working side by side; they invite each other out for coffee or lunch. You can also volunteer to join outside associations that support your work.

> ## SOCIAL MEDIA
>
> The rise of social media offers a lot of chances to get to know your coworkers better. Check out their pages on *Facebook*, *Pinterest*, and other sites to get an idea of what sorts of things they're interested in.

Understand how people individually contribute to the workplace, without making assumptions about titles and work connections. If you do find yourself making a faux pas, there are a couple of ways to make amends.

- Admit your error with sincere simplicity: "I apologize. I misspoke," or "I'm sorry, it's been that kind of day."
- Some people find it easier to admit a mistake by using humility and humor: "I'm such an idiot sometimes. I hope you'll pardon my ignorance."
- Pick a strategy to change the energy of the exchange and then proceed without beating yourself up too much.

Client Mixing

Clients have a social face and a business face. At any given time, they reflect diverse aspects of both their personal and professional personalities. Understand what it is they want from you and you succeed in being on the same wavelength in communication. The assumed boundaries in business can

SMALL TALK EXERCISE

FIGURE OUT PERSONALITIES

To know how your personality best works within any business atmosphere and what communication strategies are useful, be aware of standard business layers:

- *Corporate/company personalities*—Is the company traditional or cutting-edge, uptight or laid back? Observe interactions at the various levels: understanding interaction dynamics between secretaries/assistants and their bosses, between entry-level positions and middle management, between middle management and upper management. Who interacts well with all these levels, and who has an attitude? What is the dress code? Successfully meeting with a targeted potential client demands the same kind of research into corporate or company personality. Know thy work playmates.
- *Individual personalities*—The personalities of the people you work with have a big impact on your interactions. You meet all types of people— extroverts/introverts, go-getters/slackers, people who jump into a group dynamic with

aplomb/people who are independent thinkers and workers. Get to know what people are like as individuals.

- *Age differences*—Someone twenty-four is going to have different life experiences than someone who is fifty-four. Take age into consideration when you interact. Be sensitive to age factors. Be respectful and understand what behavior and attitudes are appropriate to people of various ages.

- *Gender differences*—Gender differences may mean adjusting your interaction style. It's not unusual to find business books that use war and sports metaphors for business, as many men are comfortable with the "business is war" concept. Women may use language more focused on relationship building and tuned-in to interaction dynamics.

be very sterile; test these limits. Engaging clients on an emotional level may help you to build your relationships.

- Figure out the drill.
- Know when to be direct and when to be diplomatic.
- Know when to be cheerfully friendly and when to be work focused.

Workplace Ethics

The business world presents plenty of occasions for testing our personal ethical nature and our ability to adhere to positive rules for behavior and to resist the negative ethics of a given workplace. Small talk will not get you very far if you aren't someone people respect. Some general rules:

- No backstabbing.
- Do not engage in petty gossip.
- Show integrity/speak the truth.
- Give employees you manage the guidance and support they need to succeed.
- Respect differences/different work styles.
- Do the right thing/don't rationalize improper behavior (there are not as many gray areas in ethical behavior as people would like to convince themselves exist).
- Appropriately recognize personnel achievements.
- Give credit where credit is due.
- Don't create "fires" to put out.

CHAPTER 7

NETWORKING WITH FLAIR

NETWORKING CAN BE an intimidating process for those who get nervous or feel out of place around strangers. Yet each new networking event is really a safe haven for making fresh connections. After all, no one has expectations about what you are like. There's no history or impressions established yet. Embrace this fact to create energy around professionally pursuing your networking goals.

When you're feeling nervous as you enter a room of strangers, enter confidently, using your body language—standing tall and smiling—to ground you in the moment. Fight any urge to flee by considering that in a networking situation you have the advantage of knowing that people in attendance expect you to approach them, to be somewhat forward, and to make the rounds.

> **BEARING GIFTS**
>
> When you come into a room to network, you come with gifts in hand—a service, a product, or personal contacts that may be beneficial to others. In this context, what you do and whom you know, along with your likable personality, are key assets that people expect you to "sell."

The Elevator Spiel

Prepare an elevator spiel for networking occasions. This is an explanation of who you are, what you do, your expertise or business philosophy, and any notable successes, brief enough in length to be shared on an elevator ride. As you network, such a prepared description can be introduced into conversation naturally either all at once or as appropriate. At some networking meetings each person is asked to stand up and introduce him- or herself. Be prepared and you will be at ease when the spotlight shines on you.

SAMPLE SPIELS

"My name is Sue Smith from San Diego. I'm an award-winning residential interior designer in business for ten years. I focus on contemporary design that features environmentally friendly and sustainable building and interior materials."

"Hi, my name is Jack Brown. I work in Seattle, connecting people with tech issues to tech folks who can help them. I particularly concentrate on people working in the hobby gaming industry and the video-game industry."

"My name is Ron Jones, and I'm a copywriter from New York City. I've written marketing copy for some of the biggest companies in the country and in the fifteen years I've been doing it I've helped firms increase their revenue by millions of dollars."

Small Talk Foraging

One friend amusingly refers to networking as foraging behavior. You seek and find communication nourishment, some to be consumed immediately and additional data to be stockpiled for later use. Effective networking benefits from small talk that encourages the outpouring of tasty information. You have pretty wide latitude here as questions can combine both business and personal aspects. Taking a business stance you might ask:

- "I haven't seen you here before. Are you new to this networking group?"
- "Are you familiar with today's speaker? The topic sounds interesting."
- "Hi, nice to meet you, Joan. I'm new to this networking group. Can you tell me what you like most about this particular group?"
- "Debra, what type of clients typically use your financial counseling services?"

Likewise, you can be more personal:

- "Joan, you live in the area, can you recommend a good restaurant for lunch?"
- "Gary, I saw you drive up in a hybrid. How do you like it?"

Embark upon networking as equal parts business and social training. To be successful you need to be prepared and approachable, focused and engaging. You should walk away with tangible results—business cards to add to your Rolodex, contacts to follow up with, and perhaps products or services sold. Concentrate on interacting genuinely, exhibit self-confidence, be in the moment, listen attentively and show interest, ask both business and personal questions, offer helpful information as the opportunity arises, and have a sense of play about the encounters.

Unhelpful Business Behavior

Business activities such as meetings, network gatherings, association assemblies, and work retreats are ideal environments for establishing your reputation, conveying your business smarts, and enlarging your realm of business contacts. Yet these same happenings can be potential danger zones for poor communication behavior. The pressures of doing business, of occasionally finding oneself not adequately prepared, and wanting desperately to shine, can bring out less than helpful behavior. Not everyone finds that she is the personification of grace under pressure. So in addition to paying attention to helpful communication tips, it's important to know what not to do as you interact.

- *Don't be question crazy.* Don't fire off questions in a nervous rat-a-tat-tat and then not give the person you're addressing a chance to answer by continuing to ask more questions. Questions are not merely dead air filler; they should come from a real sense of interest. You want to learn; you want to discover points of commonality and mutually beneficial areas for support or assistance.

- *Don't be a neurotic talker.* Save free association and monologues for the acting class. Rambling about nothing very interesting, or conversing with no point in mind will cause you to lose your listeners' attention. Try an engaging anecdote related to the topic of conversation instead.

- *Don't be a success monopolizer.* Limit your recitations of all your accomplishments and winning business strategies to a reasonable length and encourage others to relate their strengths or business history. Especially avoid turning every topic of conversation into an opening for telling others how successful you are at that particular thing. If a topic comes up that naturally enables you to relate a pertinent story, by all means share it. Just don't brag to the extreme.

- *Don't be a blank slate.* Take ownership of what you've accomplished and communicate your enthusiasm for what you do.

- *Don't be impolite.* Nerves can create energy that is difficult to harness. If you are speaking with just one person, don't interrupt or call into question a comment being made. Try to wait until they have clearly stopped talking to add your thoughts or to considerately question someone. If you are networking with a group of people, politely interject without rushing or running over the thoughts of others. Be aware of how often you speak. If someone is more reticent than the other participants, draw them out with a direct question: "Susan, tell us something about your business."

● *Don't be negative.* A good impression stems from an upbeat presence as well as positive and encouraging words. Complaining, blaming, gossiping, or confronting make poor communication pals.

The Name Game

Nearly everyone has, at some point, forgotten or been unable to recall a name, often at the most inopportune moment. These I-can't-believe-I-just-blanked-on-their-name instances are awkward on many levels. While you can't count on 100 percent recall, there are tricks that can help to bolster your name recall ability.

● *First, be fully present during that first encounter.* Make sure you give the new person your full attention—without wandering mental chatter.

● *Second, lock eyes and repeat the person's name as you respond to the introduction:* "Hi, Jake, so glad to meet you." As you talk, continue to use his name: "Jake, when did you get into town for the convention?" "Jake, is this your first time to this networking group?" If you forget the name within the initial conversation, politely ask him to repeat it one more time. Generally, this is less stressful than to have to do it the next time you run into him.

- *Use your own interests to help with recall.* If you know someone with the same name, silently reinforce this connection by saying to yourself, "Oh, Elizabeth like my cousin Elizabeth." Relate the name to someone famous or to a popular culture image if an association immediately comes to mind: Will as in *Will and Grace*, or Gwen, like Gwen Stefani. Some people lightheartedly voice the connection they are thinking of to the person they are meeting for the first time, "John Carey, any relation to Mariah Carey?" This introduction tactic provides the other person with a chance to play off the connection you made.

- *Be creative.* Some people employ rhymes to remember a name. Have fun with the rhyme so it is memorable. The rhyme may even include information about the person's profession: Sue, Sue the cosmetic guru; or Brad, Brad the restaurant comrade. You could associate the name with something the person is wearing: Heather, soft name, soft sweater. Associate the name with the person: Bob, short name, short guy; Angelina, angelic name, sweet person.

- *Create a definition for the name.* For example, Jake Brown is a satisfactory (jake) earth color (brown); Diana is a Greek goddess; or Lily is a flower. Also, you might better remember the name by categorizing it: Ty as in Ty Cobb, a sporty name; Joan as in Joan of Arc, a religious name. Associate the name with a specific ethnicity if that aspect of the name stands out: Colleen, sounds Irish; or Margot, sounds French.

Nametags provide a visual reinforcement along with the audio introduction. If you are the person initiating the contact at a networking or trade show and are looking at a nametag, take a mental picture of the name, including any other information on the nametag such as company name or location. Then say, "Hello Barbara, my name is Melissa. I see that you are from Boston." This reinforces the name and place connection and launches you into small talk such as, "Are you glad to be getting a break from the cold weather?" Some people like to covertly take in the information on a nametag, but there's nothing wrong with being obvious about it either. And, by being obvious, if any of the information is in error or the written name is their preferred moniker, the wearer is more likely to point it out. If a last name (or first) is difficult for you to pronounce simply give it a once-through and ask, "Did I pronounce that correctly?"

USE AND REUSE

Like other small talk tactics, name games become easier and more automatic with repeated use. At an initial meeting, it's most important to remember a first name, so concentrate on that if trying to recall a last name seems like too much, especially in a situation in which you are meeting many people.

Forgetting a name is never optimal, but there are strategies to help you recover as gracefully as possible. If the face looks familiar, wait to see if talking with the person for a few minutes jars your memory. You may be able to get through the conversation without needing to verbalize his name, and can then find someone to tell you his name afterwards. Sometimes it's best to simply limit your stress by admitting to your mental failing. "I'm sorry, this is a little distressing but I've forgotten your name," or "I'm embarrassed to admit that my memory isn't what it should be; could you please tell me your last name again?" Most people will understand, especially if you can recall something else about them: "I remember that you live in Philadelphia and have a teenage daughter, but I can't for the life of me recall your name."

TAKE NOTE

If the introduction is an especially important connection, make notes after a conversation or an event that will help you to remember the particulars of a person. You will be able to use the information in conversation the next time you see him or when you follow up with a note or a phone call. People are generally flattered to have others recall facts about them.

If you've forgotten a person's name and find yourself needing to introduce her to someone, introduce the person you know first and see if the mystery person will fill in her name. If she doesn't fill in the blank, you'll have to admit that her name escapes your recall: "I'd like to properly introduce you to my coworker Julie, but I'm having a bad memory day. Could you please tell me your name again?" As with all conversation, be warm and genuine and others are likely to forgive such a common lapse.

Trade Shows: Pointers for Yakking in the Aisles

What comes to mind when you think trade shows? Aching feet and an overabundance of stimuli? How about one big happy business neighborhood? After all, a trade show is essentially a metropolis composed of vendors, competitors, customers, window shoppers, amusements, and visitors. Here are some pointers to help you network at these events:

- Approach it as you would a new town. That is, comfortably, with curiosity and a sincere desire to create connections.
- Make "dates" (appointments) in advance. People's schedules at these events fill up quickly.
- Set a communication goal: know whether you are interested in a few quality contacts or want to visit (meet) as many exhibitors as possible. This enables you to be direct with the people you come in contact with about how they should interact with you: briefly and to the point, or fully engaged with more in-depth explanations. And know what you want to communicate to others, what personal and professional aspects are important to convey.

Attendees: Close and Curious Encounters

From an attendee perspective, trade show conversations can tell you many different things about a company:

- Its corporate personality
- The company's standing/reputation within the industry
- The general personality of a company's employees (are they dressed in business casual, conservatively in suits, or wearing matching clothing items such as golf shirts?)
- The inventiveness of products
- The fresh take on a needed service

For an attendee, trade show smarts include employing opening lines and questions such as:

"Hello, Joan, I understand that you are the expert on [fill in the blank as appropriate]."

"Hi, Robert. I'm Mary Smith from company X. I'd like to take a look at your new products."

"Sarah, this is my first year at this trade show and your booth caught my eye. How did you decide on this design concept for your exhibit?" (This should give you information about the company's marketing strategy and may be instructive about the company's personality. If the person doesn't know this information, you may infer that there is a serious lack of communication between departments.)

"Hello, Matthew. This show is really busy for me and I'm on a tight schedule. Could you briefly point out the key points

of your products/services that are most important for me to know?"

"Wow, you've really generated some great traffic at your booth. Who had the clever idea to put on a dance revue?"

"Emily, I like your booth, it's a real attention-getter. What can you tell me about your business?"

"Hi, Zach, can you answer a few questions for me?"

Exhibitors: Putting Communication Smarts on Display

If you are an exhibitor, you know that no single environment is more competitive than a trade show. You are competing for the very aspects that make human relations work: someone's attention, ear, interest, and desire to make a connection. You are probably familiar with the typical ploys companies and entrepreneurs use to grab attention in order to show their products or to convey a business service: scantily clad showgirls, scantily clad models conducting prizewinning games, and autograph-signing athletes. If you don't have access to obvious attention-getters, you can develop your creativity and personality to charm the masses, so to speak, by creating connection opportunities one person at a time. Consider the following trade show strategies.

1. *Disarm the people.* Stefan, president of an employee-screening firm, states that he relies on catching people's

attention with the unexpected in order to maximize the advantages of the setting. "At most trade shows, so much out of the norm is going on that you can step out of a strictly traditional role and try tactics that you wouldn't in other business settings. Sometimes I will stop a person passing by our booth by handing them a company premium and saying with a straight face, 'You just cannot leave here without this, you'll need it to get on the plane.' It's disarming enough to make them pause and laugh or make a remark like, 'Yeah, what makes this so special?' I get the opening I need to start talking business." As is true for social situations, keeping perspective and a sense of humor can work well in a trade show atmosphere, where socializing skills facilitate networking and can be conducive to conducting enjoyable business. What you don't want is to project desperation or the impression of being totally ill at ease in your surroundings. It's just not inviting and people will avoid entering such an atmosphere.

2. *The giveaway opener.* Use communication strategies that feel comfortable to you and that are a good fit for your personality. If being disarming is a stretch, don't go there. Know your audience and focus on selecting giveaways that will entice the specific conventiongoers you are targeting. Donna, a public relations expert based in New Jersey, used copies of popular anime movies to entice a high-tech audience. Participants needed to sign up for a chance to obtain a copy—providing the perfect pause to

begin small talk. "Thanks for stopping by. We're showing a new product that's almost as much fun as watching anime." Well-chosen giveaways provide a perfect buffer for comfortably leading you into business small talk. Ideally, the giveaway should either tie in to a theme/product or service feature that you are conveying at the show, or should be so universally desirable to your audience that they will generate activity and get people talking.

3. *Stop 'em with visual impact.* Can't hire the dancing bears? Try a visual that packs a punch. This could be a fabulous photograph with a catchy caption. Declare product or service benefits boldly. Partner a poster with one of those "did you know"–type statements that most people can't resist and you've created your opening line with strangers and potential customers who stop by your exhibit. Tracy, a regional sales manager for a national company, confirms that visuals do catch his eye as he walks a convention floor and that they provide an easy way to begin a conversation. "The visual gets me to stop, to investigate the product or company. Then I ask questions like 'How long have you been manufacturing this product?' or 'Has this been a good product for you?'" Likewise, Susan, a landscape architect with the National Park Service, stated that the most intriguing and alluring visuals catch her attention.

Make your brief exchange count. Take the lead if you aren't approached directly. Capture initial interest with pleasant conversation. Push your comfort boundaries while staying upbeat. And, don't exert too much pressure on the participant to respond in a particular manner that fills some invisible quota. Add to that winning formula visual stimulation, some giveaway enticements, and the distribution and exchange of useful information, and trade shows don't have to be a painful series of rejections, blank stares, and fumbling conversations.

One other thought on showing your communication savvy. Trade shows typically offer topic-specific sessions that present opportunities for networking and making good impressions upon associates and people in your industry. If you know in advance that there will be an open discussion or that participants will be encouraged to ask questions of a panel of experts, be prepared to ask a question in the most intellectual way you can.

COME PREPARED

Susan, the landscape architect, recommends: "If I'd like the answer to a specific question, or want to take the discussion in a particular direction or open it up to a controversial topic, I come prepared with a question I want to articulate well and in a polite and respectful manner. What you don't want is to come off as pedantic or to discredit yourself in front of business peers."

SMALL TALK EXERCISE

ENGAGING THE CUSTOMER

Once people come to your exhibit, be prepared to engage them in a meaningful way. If all you do is hand out freebies, without creating a personal connection or without exchanging information, you'll miss a great opportunity to get the word out and to generate leads that you can follow up afterwards. Trade shows bring prospective customers right to you, so know what you want people to remember about your booth or business.

- Do you want to convey one central theme or are you trying to sell a specific product or concept?
- Do you want to broadcast benefits that address a pervasive industry issue or would you like to make clear that customer service is your forte? Pointing out useful information found in a brochure is a nonthreatening way to involve a potential customer in conversation. Remember, use open-ended questions; they are the most engaging and tend to elicit responses that naturally lead to your next question or comment. Try opening lines and questions like the following.

"Hi, Madison, thanks for visiting us. Maybe you could share with me a little about what you are looking for?"

"I'm glad you stopped by for the raffle, Nick. Now that I've got your attention, what do you think about our products?"

"Ah, so our photograph caught your eye. What do you like best about the image?"

"Hi there. I see you reviewing our service benefits. Which benefit surprises you?"

"Thanks for making the time to stop by. Tell me something about your business needs."

"Hi, Rebecca. So what are you seeing at the show today that's making an impression?"

"Hello, Ethan. What questions can I answer for you?"

"Emma, you look like the kind of person whose opinion I would respect. We're trying to get a sense about how people feel about..." (an industry issue, the impact of a news event on consumer buying behavior, a certain product or service feature, etc.).

"Ryan, it's nice to see you again. What do you think about the booth this year?"

Tactics such as forethought and planning, physical presentation, an optimistic and confident attitude, a sincere smile and warm handshake, genuine interest and enthusiasm, a sense of humor, and telling personal stories that make you memorable boost your success rate.

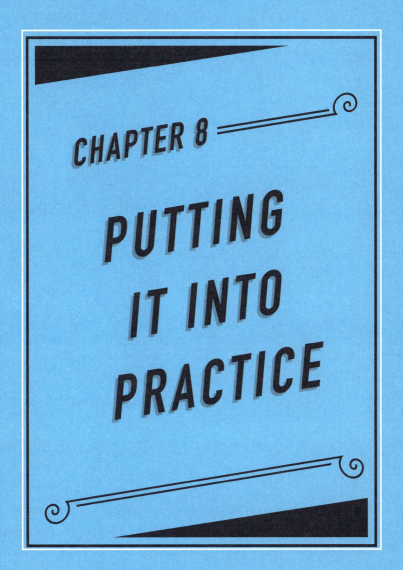

CHAPTER 8

PUTTING IT INTO PRACTICE

FINALLY, JUST ABOUT all that needs to be said about small talk has been articulated. Now you are ready to put yourself out in the world and mingle among the people. Be kind to yourself and persevere. Don't let lingering fears or frustration manifest as disinterest, ennui, or anger at others or yourself. Growth always has its awkward moments and proceeds in increments, often more slowly than we'd like. Watch for the small and significant advances, such as:

- An evolving attitude about socializing (i.e., from hating it to nervous trial and error, from self-conscious participation to eagerly searching out social opportunities)
- Gradually feeling more comfortable in your own skin, and more forgiving of occasional flubs
- Body language awareness tuning you into others' attitudes and reactions
- Increased confidence in new situations
- A playful manner activating instances of lighthearted banter
- An expanding personal world as a result of adding informational texture and color to daily life
- "Aha" moments of understanding when conversation tactics work
- Dialogue skills boosting the enjoyment quotient of dating
- Social risk-taking and spontaneity increasing/enhancing your social network
- Improved communication smarts at work resulting in an enhanced business image

Over time, the potential for personal growth is huge! And, with time being the swift flier that it is, before long you'll feel like a community member of the world. No longer will you feel as if being shy or introverted is a barrier to things you desire to accomplish and people you'd like to meet. How much fun is that?

The Social Mind Self-Assessment

All action stems from a particular attitude, a certain mindset that is part of our personality at any given time. We can change the results we get by altering our expectations and our focus. Let's see where you are today. Answer yes or no to the following statements.

1. My attitude about making new connections is generally positive.
2. I'm less blasé or negative about going out socially.
3. I am in charge of my self-confidence.
4. I can anticipate a time when small talk will be natural for me.
5. I honestly believe that a sense of humor will help me in small talk.
6. I plan to work on projecting a positive presence.
7. It's okay to be nervous; it's good energy I can use.
8. Diversifying and enhancing my interests will be fun.
9. Social ease is equal parts exposure, expenditure, and experience.

10. I'm more interested in face-to-face encounters than electronic relationships.
11. I've taken stock of my strengths and personal assets.
12. Already, I'm more observant of others and my surroundings.
13. I'm trying to be more spontaneous.
14. My listening skills have improved.
15. I can name two body language cues that help others know that I am interested in them.
16. I'm trying not to predetermine the results of my social interactions.
17. I believe that the (learning) process is as important as the result.
18. I've pinpointed areas to make small talk advances (attitude, conversational style, better listening, personal revelation, eye contact, having topics in mind, etc.).
19. I have the lead role in determining my relationship successes.
20. I've tried some of the small talk prompts.

If you answered 1–5 yes: Either you don't believe everything you read or you're not sure you have what it takes to overcome your social weaknesses. Try anyway. Let action stand in for confidence for a while. Focus on one area of your life that could benefit from enhanced social skills. Try some of the suggested exercises consistently for two or three months.

If you answered 6–10 yes: The spirit is willing but the mind has a few lingering doubts and, perhaps, the body hasn't quite kicked into high gear. As you try the tactics, paying attention to tips for building positive communication skills (as well as ineffective behavior), your emotional, mental, and physical sides should start to harmonize. Take one step at a time and keep progressing. As needed, refer back to the book to refresh yourself on specific strategies. This is a work in progress.

If you answered 11–15 yes: You have the right attitude. Now all you need are new experiences and a track record of small successes in order to gently persuade yourself that you're fully in charge of this portion of your life. It only gets better from here on out.

If you answered 16–20 yes: You're ready to be a small talk pro! Your commitment to making this work for an enhanced social experience should help make the process enjoyable.

Building Small Talk Assets

As we've discussed, no person is one thing all the time (whether it's shy or outgoing, unsure or confident), and no one person is defined by one personality trait. Just as some days we're more moody or energetic, there are times when we just feel more social. Fortunately, we have each new day in front of us to try something new, to change an attitude or action that's not working. Concentrate on building small talk assets rather than trying to dismantle perceived negative aspects of one's self. Positive actions will create positive reactions in your life. Take the following true-or-false quiz to further measure your small talk know-how.

➤ SMALL TALK KNOW-HOW: TRUE-OR-FALSE QUIZ

1. If I don't make a positive first impression the relationship potential is doomed.
   ❏ **True**   ❏ **False**

2. The best assets to bring to a social event are: a sense of humor, self-confidence, and realistic expectations.
   ❏ **True**   ❏ **False**

3. It's better to lie if you're not interesting.
   ❏ **True**   ❏ **False**

4. Only shy people get nervous in the public eye.
   ❏ **True**   ❏ **False**

5. The Four Ps of dating are: plan, preen, persevere, and pop the question.
   ❏ **True**   ❏ **False**

6. An open-ended question means that the person can choose whether or not to answer you.
   ❏ **True**   ❏ **False**

7. A smile is a great tool for deception.
   ❏ **True**   ❏ **False**

8. If I act busy people will think that I have an interesting life.
   ❏ **True**   ❏ **False**

9. At-home entertaining and business meals are a wonderful way to nourish relationships.
   ❏ **True**   ❏ **False**

10. In business, good topics are the weather, current events, industry news, family, and humorous personal stories.
    ❏ **True**   ❏ **False**

➤ ANSWERS

1. *False.* Yes, first impressions are ideal, but small talk skills such as self-deprecating humor, body awareness, a warm smile, and "interested" questions can get most anyone past a few awkward first moments.

2. *True.* There are many personal assets you can "bring to the party," but this dynamic trio especially assures that your social interactions will flow naturally and be enjoyable.

3. *False.* Lying is inauthentic. It's better to use your energy to actually be interesting than to waste energy covering for false information.

4. *False.* Nearly everyone has moments of nervousness. The key is to reduce nervousness with planning and enhanced communication skills, as well as to translate nervousness into an uplifting energy during interchanges.

5. *False.* The Four Ps of dating are: plan, primp, project, and promote.

6. *False.* An open-ended question requires more than a yes or no answer, helping to fuel conversation and elicit meaningful answers.

7. *False.* A smile is a great social skill to put others at ease, but it must be genuine or it will come across as a "fake front."

8. *False.* People are more likely to think that you overextend yourself or feel that you don't have room in your life for new friends and activities. Neither is conducive to growing your social or work contacts.

9. *True.* Making people feel welcome reflects positively on you—new acquaintances feel good about being included

and friendships are reinforced. Business-related meals tend to make people more relaxed and open, setting the stage for conversation and relationship building.

10. *True.* Many of the same topics used in social situations can be used in business, in addition to work-related topics.

The Celebration Checklist

Remember, people who truly enjoy connecting with other people tend to have a wider connection to the banquet of life offerings. Consciously or unconsciously, they use many of the tactics discussed in *How to Make Small Talk*. Be open to new experiences. Find the fun in small talk. As you experiment with small talk strategies and have success, keep track of them. Here is a checklist of successes that may be celebrated.

- ❏ I opened myself up to two new social opportunities this month (a new club, neighborhood art walk, book club, etc.).
- ❏ Friends commented on me being more outgoing.
- ❏ My discomfort level when meeting new people has lessened.
- ❏ I used two "did you know" questions today.
- ❏ I had a conversation with someone different from me (in terms of looks, intellectual pursuits, lifestyle, etc.).
- ❏ I interviewed myself prior to an important social event.
- ❏ I'm consciously trying to be a good listener.
- ❏ I initiated a conversation that resulted in a date/a new friend.

- ❏ I'm cultivating curiosity about others and the world.
- ❏ I'm better at verbalizing compliments to others rather than just thinking them.
- ❏ I've gotten to know two people in my neighborhood.
- ❏ I hosted a dinner party, cocktail party, themed party, or holiday get-together.
- ❏ I made a point of talking with my _____ [Fill in the blank: mail carrier/post office clerk, grocery clerk, restaurant waiter/owner/chef, dry cleaner, coffee shop patrons, etc.].
- ❏ I made the first move to speak to someone new/to extend an invitation.
- ❏ I've explored retail stores in my town, introducing myself to the people working there.
- ❏ I extended spontaneous invitations to neighbors or coworkers for [circle appropriate activities] coffee, breakfast, lunch, a glass of wine, a leisure activity.
- ❏ I regularly go where people gather.
- ❏ I joined a professional association or networking group.
- ❏ I used a name game successfully.
- ❏ I've participated in a [circle appropriate activities] charity group function, spiritual-related group activity, arts or entertainment organization event, alumni group activity, sporting team activity (softball game, bike club ride), cultural organization event, etc.
- ❏ I'm enriching my life with a class or how-to seminar, etc.
- ❏ I accepted an invitation I would have turned down last year.
- ❏ My boss complimented me on my proactive participation.

- ❏ I'm getting to know my coworkers better.
- ❏ I did a better job connecting and following up with people I met at a work event.
- ❏ I prepared an introduction for myself that adequately reflects my accomplishments.
- ❏ I was a personable/outgoing person today.

These are just a few of the many accomplishments that should add up as you refine your small talk capabilities. As you practice projecting a cheerful and inviting attitude, and use body language to radiate ease and confidence, you will find all the components of effective interchange becoming more automatic.

Keeping Track of Small Talk Specifics

Make a point of recalling what goes right for you in social and business encounters. Keep a notebook or journal that tracks some of the finer points of conversation. It not only reinforces success, it also helps you to better recall what doesn't work. Social entries might include the following:

- Most successful/least successful opening lines to date
- Interesting topics discussed
- Well-received jokes/jokes that fell flat
- "In the news" or entertainment information brought up successfully
- Situations in which self-deprecating humor was useful

- Interesting replies to questions
- Insights you've gleaned about yourself
- Good questions asked by other people
- Body language cues/mannerisms observed in others (and in what particular situations)
- Favorite place(s) to meet new people
- Small talk skills you've noticed other people use
- Topics you'd like to learn more about
- Actions that still feel unnatural
- Traits of good communicators/speakers

Remember, no one gets business interaction right all the time. Even superconfident, self-proclaimed business "smarties" make basic communication errors. Awareness and common sense, being genuine and checking in with others, speaking and acting with integrity, and engaging others in a timely and helpful manner are key to effective workplace communication. It's vital to your progress to be aware of and note what communication successes you experience related to work. Suggested business-related developments to track:

- Progress you perceive in any specific business area (easier interactions with superiors, helpful actions in regards to coworkers, more confidence in meetings, successful mediation of a challenging work situation, strengthening of a client relationship, etc.)
- Comments made by others that indicate they perceive a positive difference (note in what area: general

performance, communication effectiveness, approach-ability, friendliness, proactive participation, etc.)

- Wider circle of positive coworker connections
- New business-related newsletters or professional journals you are reading
- A communication skill you learned from being observant of someone else
- Beneficial networking connections
- Work insights or education (or certification) received from taking a course or class
- Letters, memos, or verbal input from clients commending attentive and/or effective interactions
- Proactive behavior that resulted in a positive outcome for self or company

Not only is this information supportive of your progress and good for building your self-confidence, it can be used for things such as self-evaluations that many companies request prior to review time, and in promotion or interview conversations.

Conversational Cheat Sheet

Conversation dynamics can be simplified by remembering that certain attitudes and actions are conducive to positive exchanges:

1. Exhibit genuine curiosity about people and an interest in connecting with them
2. Breathe: to stay in the moment and relax

3. Smile: the warm energy of a smile is contagious
4. Inject levity: don't take yourself too seriously and show a sense of humor
5. Listen well: to show respect and to learn
6. Engage others: get people to talk about themselves
7. Play off environmental stimuli: conversation topics lie in furniture, design, people, specific actions, clothes, food, wine, etc.
8. Display empathy and understanding: let people know you relate and/or hear their point of view
9. Show self: indicate commonalities as well as share your history and your interests
10. Be giving: offer helpful advice or information, and be responsible for contributing your share to conversation success

Scenarios

As we've made clear, your small talk abilities will be raised in all kinds of diverse situations. The more you practice these abilities, the more natural your conversational skills will seem, both to you and to others. Now that you've mastered the general principles of small talk, here are some circumstances in which you can exercise your small talk muscles:

Example #1: The Work Party

Context: There's a small social gathering at your workplace to celebrate a coworker's promotion. About twenty people are present. Because you're comparatively new to the company, there are a number of people at the event whom you either don't know or don't know very well.

➤ CONVERSATIONAL PROMPTS

- "Hi. I'm _____. I just joined the company a month and a half ago, working on [some recent project you've been involved with]. What do you do?"
- "Hi. I'm _____, and I'm a bit new here. Can you tell me who some of these people are and what they do?"
- "It sure is great about [coworker]'s promotion. How much does the company promote from within, versus hiring from outside?"

➤ CONVERSATIONAL DON'TS

- "Sure must be nice to be [promoted coworker]. Wonder if the rest of us will ever get a promotion." (This sets a negative tone for the conversation.)
- "Does the company always promote from within?" (A yes or no question that can end the conversation before it really gets going.)

Example #2: The Neighborhood Cook-Out

Context: Every year in your neighborhood, people get together for a cook-out. Everyone brings food and mingles. You know most of the people there, but you've never found it easy to talk to them.

● "Hi, Janice! I noticed that you had a tree service over the other day to take down those two big evergreens. What was the problem with them? And what did you think of the service?"

● "Carl and Anne! You guys have great tans. Where'd you go on your vacation this year?"

● "I saw you folks are using a new trash pick-up service. What do you think of them?"

● "The new paint job on the house looks great! What made you go with that color?"

● "Someone told me you brought these Parmesan French fries. They're great! Where'd you get the recipe?"

➤ CONVERSATIONAL DON'TS

● "Here comes Earl. Have you guys heard about the reason his wife left him?" (Gossip is never an attractive quality, and it's even worse in a neighborhood, where it can spread and grow, causing local feuds.)

● "Geez! Who brought the potato salad? It smells as if it's been sitting in the sun half the day." (This is going to be peculiarly embarrassing if the person who brought potato salad turns out to be the one you're talking to. Keep things positive.)

Example #3: Out on a Date

Context: You've set up a date through an Internet dating service. You're eating dinner at a nice restaurant, one your date suggested, in an informal setting. The waiter has just taken your drink order.

➤ CONVERSATIONAL PROMPTS

- "This place seems very nice. What sort of food do you like when you go out?"
- "I'm glad you recommended this restaurant, since I just moved to the area recently and I don't know a lot of places. Why do you like it?"
- "What sorts of things do you like to do in your spare time? Are you into indoor or outdoor activities?"
- "You said that you've just started a new job. What is it you do now? What kind of training does that take?"

➤ CONVERSATIONAL DON'TS

- "That wine you ordered won't go very well with the entrée you were talking about ordering." (Nobody likes a know-it-all, especially not one who criticizes your choice in food or wine on a first date.)
- "This place seems a little pricey. Are you sure this was really the best choice?" (Cheapskates don't usually get second dates, particularly ones who blame the choice of restaurant on their companion.)

Example #4: At the Local Pet Fair

Context: There's a pet fair going on in your town. Since you've only moved there comparatively recently, it's a great opportunity to network and meet people with similar interests. You're not exhibiting any of your pets, just walking around the show, looking at the animals and talking to the owners.

➤ CONVERSATIONAL PROMPTS

● "What an interesting-looking dog! He looks like a cross between a Maltese and a dachshund. Can you tell me some more about him?"

● "That's such an interesting name for a cat. Can you tell me, what was your thinking behind it?"

● "There seem to be a lot of people here today. Where do most of them at the show come from? It seems as if people in this area are really into their pets."

● "I've just moved to the area and I'm very into animals. In _____ where I lived before, I volunteered at a couple of animal shelters. What are some of the shelters around here that need volunteers? Which ones would you recommend?"

➤ CONVERSATIONAL DON'TS

● "The shows I went to in the last town I lived in were bigger than this." (This sort of gratuitous boasting is likely to earn you an awkward silence and some irritated glances.)

● "I like the dogs they're showing here, but I can't stand cats. They're so sneaky and mean. It's too bad they have both of them here." (Refrain from being judgmental or opinionated. Besides, the person you're talking to may be a passionate cat lover.)

The Outcome of All This Blathering

In the end, the result you desire from acquiring small talk confidence should be simple: you want to feel good about yourself and your interaction with others. You achieve this by following through on your intention to meet people, by resolving to be yourself, and to have a good time.

Over time, one new connection at a time, small talk improvements should inspire progressive and powerful thoughts such as: "New situations stimulate me in a good way," "I enjoy being engaged with the world outside my job/home/current social circle," "I'm feeling more cheerful than nervous," and "I'm an interesting person." You may even notice that people are letting you know in various ways that you are having a positive impact on their lives. And that is truly the mark of success for any relationship. So keep small talking!

APPENDIX: CONVERSATION PROMPTS

IN ADDITION TO the prompts included with the scenarios we outlined earlier, here are some other general prompts you can use in starting and continuing small talk. Remember to keep your small talk simple and keep it real. Try any of the following lines and questions (listed in no particular order) as appropriate, and at your discretion. Some are surface starter lines, while others are good probing questions that you can use as you get further along in conversation or a relationship. Remember: use your observation skills, sense of curiosity, and specific knowledge to stimulate small talk.

- "It's a beautiful day. Aren't you glad to be out enjoying it?"
- "What are you reading?"
- "What movies have you seen lately?"
- "What's your favorite food?"
- "What kind of music do you enjoy?"
- "What traits do you most admire in men/women?"
- "What's on your to-do list before you die?"

- "Is there a talent that you wish you had?"
- "What are some of your favorite movies?"
- "What has been your proudest moment?"
- "Who do you think had a really great (or well-lived) life?"
- "I can't wait for spring. What's your favorite time of year?"
- "I just read about a _____ [fill in the description]. What is your favorite invention or gadget?"
- "What do you like to do in your downtime?"
- "What kind of work do you do? Do you enjoy it?"
- "What's your dream job?"
- "Do you go to hear speakers very often?"
- "Isn't this a nice party?"
- "It was so thoughtful of _____ [fill in the name] to organize this event. I'm really enjoying it."
- "If you could live somewhere else, where would you live?"
- "Name some adjectives that you think best describe you."
- "Who in your life is most important to you?"
- "Do you have a hero?"
- "Do tell…what's your most embarrassing moment?"
- "Do you have the time?"
- "Great hairstyle. Where do you go to get it done?"
- "You had a little rush there. Is it always so busy?" (to a shop owner/employee)
- "I love your store. Where do you find such beautiful things?"
- "Where did you grow up?"
- "What is your idea of bliss?"
- "What would you do with a million dollars?"

- "I overheard your interesting conversation. It made me think of…" or "I think that you're right…" or "Is that true?" (Good prompt for those times you are in line, waiting at a doctor's office, sitting next to people at a social or entertainment event, etc. If you find what others have to say of interest, decide whether it is appropriate to join in on the conversation.)
- "This weather is gloomy. How do you cope with all the rain?"
- "Beautiful dog. What is the breed?"
- "I've never bought loose tea before. Could you explain the differences in your green teas?"
- "I've been watching you and am fascinated. What are you doing? It looks interesting."

➤ FAVORABLE TOPICS
- Food
- Hobbies
- Films
- Books
- Sports
- Travel
- Interesting articles
- Current news
- What's "hot" or "in"

➤ FOR CLOSE FRIENDS
- Politics
- Religion
- Medical problems
- Marriage concerns
- Relationship concerns
- Child problems

INDEX

ABOUT THE AUTHOR

MELISSA WADSWORTH is an introvert who found her voice first through a career in public relations and then as an inspirational speaker and personal growth workshop leader. The founder of Brilliance Unlimited, LLC, Melissa believes that finding the joy in heart-based communication, creativity, and intuition is the key sensitive people worldwide need to manifest amazing and satisfying life journeys. Learn more at her website, CollectiveManifestation.com.